What Women Are Saying Who Have Completed *Encountering the Healing Power of Forgiveness*

– "My forgiveness toward others affects much more than just me."

– "[I was reminded] of how my choice to forgive is a reflection of my trust in God."

– "This study has been life-changing!"

– "So many times He spoke through His Word straight to my heart. I love Shawn's commentary. Wonderful to feel her walking alongside me! Much, much blessed!"

– "Through the study I learned that forgiveness is more about my relationship to Christ as opposed to my relationship with the person [who has hurt me]."

– "[I learned to strive] to live in ongoing forgiveness and to know I don't have the right to judge. I want to [and can] leave a legacy for future generations because I choose to forgive."

– "[I learned] the importance of showing compassion and mercy – there is a reason for [others'] hurt and pain."

– "God really opened my eyes to ways that I was withholding forgiveness (even small, petty ways I wasn't aware of)."

– "I very much enjoyed how the study tied the four generations together and showed the spiritual and historical significance of godliness and ungodliness."

Living with Unmet Desires

ENCOUNTERING THE HEALING POWER OF FORGIVENESS

Shawn Lantz

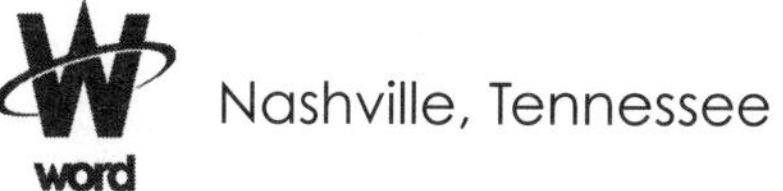

Nashville, Tennessee

Distributed by Word Books

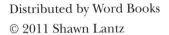

Author photo on back cover courtesy of Chris Smith of Chris and Cami Photography, Charleston, South Carolina. www.chrisandcamiphotography.com

Book cover, interior formatting and design courtesy of Allegra Network of Plymouth, Michigan. www.allegranetwork.com.

DEDICATION

My beloved is radiant and ruddy, distinguished among ten thousand.

– Song of Solomon 5:10 (ESV)

To my wonderful husband, Rob:

Over the last eighteen years of being your wife, I have had the joy of experiencing a depth of love that I did not imagine I would ever know. I am not talking about the kind of Hollywood infatuation between a man and woman that is wrongly labeled as love until they tire of the relationship. I am referring to a sort of love that is self-sacrificing, protective, and faithful. This love has propelled you to get up at 3:00 a.m. to assure one of our frightened children that daddy is there. This love puts your needs last and does not allow the words *I quit* to be part of your vocabulary.

Forgiveness – you have taught me what the word means. You married a frightened woman with a broken heart who was scared, at first, to love you like I longed to. Out of my insecurity, I would push away and in your steadfastness, you patiently said, "Bring it on! I am not going anywhere." You are the person I trust more than anyone else on earth. You are the person I want to be with the most – the one I want to grow old with. You have protected, encouraged, and given wings to my dreams. You are my hero.

I am blessed beyond what I can express to belong to such a great man. This book is as much yours as it is mine. I know that your greatest desire is for Jesus Christ to be glorified through our lives. This, more than all the wonderful qualities you possess, continues to make our marriage a safe place to grow together. I am so thankful that He gave you to me, my beloved Ohndah.

You are distinguished among ten thousand ... and you are all mine!

I love you with all of my heart,

Shawn's Gratitude List

I owe so much to the following persons for their encouragement and support:

My Lord Jesus Christ: Thank You for mercy I don't deserve. Thank You for Your complete forgiveness and reconciliation which allow me to silence the lies of the enemy as I walk in the purpose You have for me. May I never walk anywhere You do not lead. *Were the whole realm of nature mine, that were a present far too small. Love so amazing, so divine, demands my soul, my life, my all. – Isaac Watts*

My best and dearest companion, Rob: Thank you for taking my hand as we have gone from safe to faith in this ministry God has given us together. I love you with all of my heart.

My wonderful children, Chase, Jordyn, and Jenna: I pray that you will become expert forgivers and that you will follow Jesus with all of your hearts. God has taught me so much through you. I love you so much.

My parents, Jim and Nancy Smith: Thank you for the example of your lives which speaks louder than any words. Your obedience to Jesus has given me strength to continue when the road is long and difficult. I rise up and call you both blessed.

My wonderful in-laws, Jack and Helen Lantz: You amaze me by your refusal to bear grudges and your desire to forgive others. Thank you for making me feel like a daughter these last eighteen years. I love you!

My siblings, nieces, and nephews: I love you.

My sister-in-law, Karen: We have walked this road of forgiveness and reconciliation together. Look what God has done! I love you.

My Word family: Thank you to Tim, Dusty, John, Todd, and Ricky for the opportunity to serve the Lord with you by making resources available for women to fall in love with Jesus.

My FHBC pilot group: Thank you for being brave and transparent as we worked through the life of Joseph and our own struggles with forgiveness and reconciliation. I walked away the most blessed by our time together.

Dr. Andrew Schmutzer: Thank you for bringing Joseph and his family to life in a new way through your lectures. God has done deep healing in me because of the road He has asked you to walk and your willingness to share your insights with others.

To Jackie McClure and Michelle Reska of Allegra Network: Thank you for making black words on a white page look so beautiful. You have made the process a delight. Thank you for your creative talent which makes a hard topic of study beautiful in its presentation.

My wonderful participants: You are the reason for this study. I pray that Jesus would walk so closely beside you as we grapple with some of life's deepest hurts in the light of His Word. Although I may never meet you in person, the Lord has allowed me to see your faces in my mind's eye as the inspiration for the eight weeks we will spend together. I come to you, not as an expert, but as a fellow sojourner. Thank you for taking this journey with me as we ask the Lord to allow us to encounter the healing power of forgiveness.

CONTENTS

Living With Unmet Desires:

Encountering the Healing Power of Forgiveness

Introduction 9

Week One
Uncovering the Poison 11

Week Two
A House Divided 37

Week Three
A Hard Journey Home 62

Week Four
Trail of Tears 87

Week Five
Dark Night of the Soul 113

Week Six
High Places 140

Week Seven
The Plan of Glory 165

Week Eight
Reconciliation's Requirements 191

Salvation
Letter from Shawn 218

End Notes 219

INTRODUCTION

Forgiveness

I can't remember the first time I heard the story of Joseph, because I was very young. I accepted Jesus Christ as my Savior when I was five years old. Sitting cross-legged in front of a flannel graph board in Sunday School, I watched as Joseph received his multi-colored coat from his elderly father, Jacob. That scene encapsulated the story for me as a young child.

My struggle to understand what biblical forgiveness looks like began when I was in my adolescence. I became convinced that it was appropriate to hold grudges when I had been wronged. I never comprehended the link between my lack of forgiveness and the lukewarm state of my spiritual life. I believed that if I forgave someone who had deeply hurt me, I would be condoning their hurtful actions toward me, so I tenaciously clung to my bitterness.

This study is the result of a twenty-year journey with my amazing Jesus. I have weaved my own struggle with forgiveness and what He has taught me in the pages of this study. You will see that I am not an expert in the area of forgiveness. I fail often, but what I love so much about Christ is that He never makes us look at all of our sin at once. I believe He knows its full revelation would crush and discourage us. Instead, He is patient, gentle, *and* firm, and lavish in His healing. Only by His supernatural power in my life have I been able to slowly let go on the vice-grip I once had on the hurt that stemmed from my withholding forgiveness. I have learned something revolutionary in the process:

Forgiveness benefits me far more than it benefits the one I am forgiving!

Joseph's story in the book of Genesis encompasses much more than an exchange of a multi-colored coat between a son and his father. If you have ever thought the Bible to be boring, then the study of four generations of Joseph's family will change your outlook. We are going to be examining the lives of the family through whom Jesus Christ, the Savior of the world, would one day be born. Their story will run the gamut of human emotions. As the Word of God unfolds, we will be stunned at the levels of betrayal, forgiveness, and redemption that we encounter throughout this eight-week journey together.

Come along with me as God shows off His glory in a breathtaking way through the lives of ordinary, fallible human beings, just like you and me. I am so privileged to have you as my companion in the magnificent Word of God.

I have prayed this over all who would take this study:

Heal me, O LORD, and I will be healed;
save me and I will be saved,
for you are the one I praise.
Jeremiah 17:14

I praise Jesus Christ that this can be our story, too, as we ask Him to allow us to encounter the healing power of forgiveness.

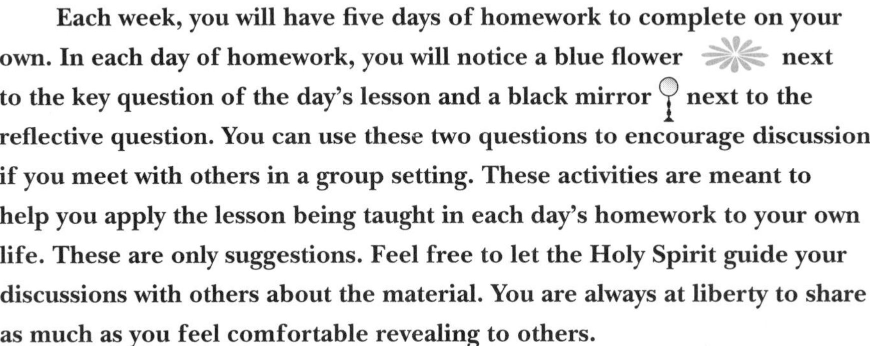

Each week, you will have five days of homework to complete on your own. In each day of homework, you will notice a blue flower next to the key question of the day's lesson and a black mirror next to the reflective question. You can use these two questions to encourage discussion if you meet with others in a group setting. These activities are meant to help you apply the lesson being taught in each day's homework to your own life. These are only suggestions. Feel free to let the Holy Spirit guide your discussions with others about the material. You are always at liberty to share as much as you feel comfortable revealing to others.

Be glorified, Lord Jesus, and speak to each of our hearts!

Uncovering The Poison

I remember the frightening afternoon when I found my eighteen-month-old brother, Jack, holding a familiar amber-colored bottle in one hand with pink drool around his lips. Sticky, smeared pills that he had spit out of his mouth lay strewn around him. Jack had found the candy-coated anti-malarial medicine our family took each week in the Congo. Jack was too young to realize that the enticing sweetness of the pills hid the bitter taste of what could be poisonous and lethal to his small body. My mind raced in horror at the thought of the possible consequences to my brother's health as my mother tried to figure out if Jack had actually eaten the poison.

Someone once said that withholding forgiveness is like you and me drinking poison and wishing our offender would die, even though we were the ones who drank the lethal substance. When you and I allow an unforgiving spirit to consume and control our thoughts and actions toward our offender, we, like my younger brother, can be ignorant of the reality that ingesting poisonous thoughts of bitterness and revenge, which will ultimately destroy us.

This first week of study is going to give us the opportunity to cry out to the Lord to help us uncover the reasons why we may be struggling to forgive, including a eye-opening look back at our family tree to see if the patterns of withholding forgiveness and other ungodly behaviors have been part of our heritage for generations. We will study choices made in the lives of Abraham, Isaac, and Jacob this week to see how recurring sins showed up in each of the three generations. I am praying that looking over their shoulders will allow us to take an honest look at the decisions that have been made in our own families.

May the Lord bless you this week, my sweet friend, as we ask Him to uncover the poison of strongholds that do not let us walk in the abundant life that Jesus promised us is ours.

One more thing ... I am happy to let you know that Jack is a healthy, married man with four children of his own today!

Day One – A Brave First Step

I have always been fascinated with cemeteries. Any cemetery. The older the cemetery, the better. The town in which I live has the oldest private Confederate soldier cemetery in the country. I could spend the better part of the day looking through the rows and rows of tombstones which are grouped there. I love reading the one line epitaphs on the blocks of granite as they rise toward the sky. It does not matter that I have never met the person buried six feet below me; my imagination loves to envision what that person was like in life. Curiosity leads me to wonder what life experiences shaped the deceased person. Sometimes the tombstone will read, *Beloved wife and mother.* Those words will lead my mind down the path of imagination as I try to envision what sort of a woman she must have been like to cause her family to etch those words on the final earthly monument to a life now gone and forgotten by many. Perhaps I secretly wonder if such words would ever be written about me by those who were closest to me during the days I spent on earth.

A cemetery is a safe and removed place to envision the past of someone who was not part of my own life. The interaction is one-sided. The person can be anyone I want them to be in my mind, even if the fantasy I have created resembles no truth to who that individual was in real life. All of my imagining can remain idyllic and lovely with no messy, dysfunctional interruptions to mar my made-up images of that person.

Although there may be a great deal of mystery as to why certain members of my family acted in ways that they did, I cannot easily be an objective person because I am part of the story line.

It is a less comfortable, more frightening exercise to analyze my own family line. Although there may be a great deal of mystery as to why certain members of my family acted in ways that they did, I cannot easily be an objective person because I am part of the story line.

There are some who do not believe in looking at the past. They believe that what is over and done with is not relevant to life today. However, every family has some skeleton in the closet somewhere. Some of the following family situations are examples: the unmarried daughter who was sent away during her pregnancy decades ago because she who brought shame to the family name. The cousin whose name is never mentioned because of the jail sentence he is currently serving for a crime he committed over twenty years ago. The suicide of the brother who was a drug addict and got lost somewhere in his adolescence. The death of the baby who is now, spoken of in almost hallowed terms by the mother who deals with the intensity of her grief as though it happened yesterday and the sibling who lives constantly in the shadow of someone he or she barely remembers or never knew.

So what do cemeteries and looking at long-buried family skeletons in the closet have to do with a Bible study on the biblical character of Joseph and forgiveness? We will spend the next weeks of this study uncovering the deep connections among these seemingly random subjects. We can only accomplish this by using the inerrant and final authority on all life's matters – the Word of God.

What do the following verses from Psalm 119 reveal that the Word of God does for us in our search for truth?

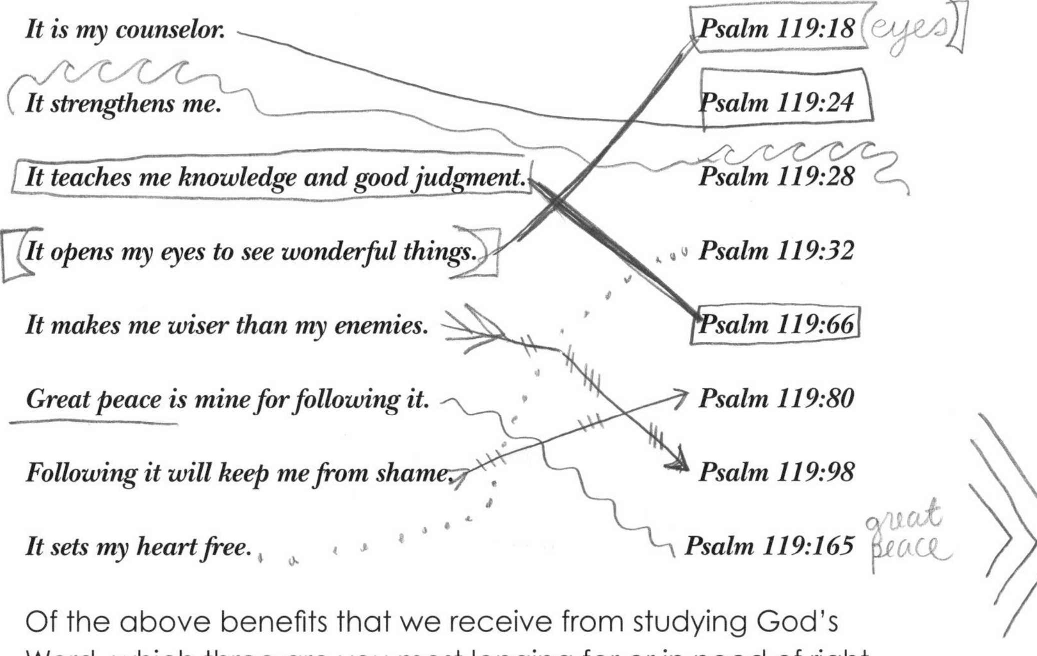

It is my counselor.	**Psalm 119:18**
It strengthens me.	**Psalm 119:24**
It teaches me knowledge and good judgment.	**Psalm 119:28**
It opens my eyes to see wonderful things.	**Psalm 119:32**
It makes me wiser than my enemies.	**Psalm 119:66**
Great peace is mine for following it.	**Psalm 119:80**
Following it will keep me from shame.	**Psalm 119:98**
It sets my heart free.	**Psalm 119:165**

Of the above benefits that we receive from studying God's Word, which three are you most longing for or in need of right now in your life? Why?

Keep me from Shame! Verse 80. I'm

because tempted to follow the lusts / my heart and need to put God first.

because Great peace. I need great peace to deal with the dad-leaving/gone situation.

because My counselor. I need counsel for all areas/life: ministry, friends, purpose, fulfilment, next job, finding a man (dating). LOVE growing in love for others. evangelism?

Scripture is clear that sinful choices made in the lives of our parents, grandparents and great-grandparents can have a profound effect on our lives today.

Please read Jeremiah 32:17-19. What does verse 18 say about sins in families?

Children inherit their parents sins in their laps.

Scripture is clear that sinful choices made in the lives of our parents, grandparents and great-grandparents can have a profound effect on our lives today. Choices that I had nothing to do with, perhaps made long before I ever arrived on the scene. Depending on what those choices were, that realization could make me feel depressed as I raise my own three children, but God, in His mercy, also made another promise to us about the reward of living lives of obedience to Him.

What do the following Scriptures tell us?

Deuteronomy 7:9:

Psalm 103:17-18:

Why have you decided to do this study on forgiveness? What are you hoping to learn specifically (you will not be asked to share this with anyone)?

We are going to look at some crucial decisions that the three generations who preceded Joseph made to help us uncover the root of dysfunction that nearly destroyed the family through whom God had said would bless all the nations of the earth. I am begging God to help us uncover our own broken places that have been hidden away from the light of His healing for too long. We are going back three generations to try to understand, with the Holy Spirit's help, why forgiveness was a singularly monumental act of grace on the part of Joseph toward those who caused him such great personal heartache and destruction.

The Bible will help us gain supernatural insight to understand past events, unlock dark secrets, and provide the opportunity to start the healing process of forgiveness.

What do you think the following statement means?

"Those who cannot remember the past are condemned to repeat it." [1]

– George Santayana

I started my first diary when I was ten years old. If you would look at that little book today, with its now yellowed pages, you would see the remains of pages that I cut out. My diary fell into the hands of someone who read those pages and teased me unmercifully over their contents. At eleven years old, I naively thought if I removed what had brought me shame, I would not remember the pain of the embarrassment I had suffered. Although I can't remember the exact words I used, I can remember clearly enough what I had written on those pages that were not meant for anyone else's eyes but mine.

It is never easy to look at pain in our pasts. This study will require us to be brave. Pain without perspective is wasted pain and is destructive to ourselves and others. That is why we will immerse ourselves in God's Word. The Bible will help us gain supernatural insight to understand past events, unlock dark secrets, and provide the opportunity to start the healing process of forgiveness.

So how do we begin? What brave step does Jeremiah 33:3 challenge us to do? Write the verse out here:

What requirement is necessary for the one brave enough to take God up on this challenge? Circle one:

Maturity	Superior intelligence	Calling to Him
Wisdom	Sinless life	

Just one requirement is needed, my sweet sister. Just one. It's not maturity. We will never be so mature that we do not have to pray for more maturity. It's not superior intelligence. I surely would not classify myself in that category. Wisdom? I find myself appalled at the unwise choices I make everyday. Sinless life? There was only one Person who lived a sinless life – Jesus Christ. Not you and me.

But you and I can call to Him. We do not need maturity, superior intelligence, wisdom, or the impossible-to-attain sinless life to ask for our God to come meet us in our need. We only need to humble ourselves and call to Him.

Forgiveness is not a one-time act; it is a process.

What is the two-part promise in Jeremiah 33:3 which will happen in our hearts when we call to Him?

1) He will ________________ us.

2) He will show us ________________ that we ________________.

Other versions of the Bible translate **unsearchable** with these words: *hidden, mysterious, mighty, secrets, and wondrous.*

The reason I choose to participate in a Bible study is generally because I need to have an answer to a particular question which it addresses. I need to have hidden facts come to light through God's Word. I need to see my circumstances, not through my feelings and emotions, but through the sifting of truth. I write a Bible study out of my desperation to know what I did not know before and what I could not possibly have knowledge of had the Lord not revealed that knowledge to me in His Word.

I can hardly think of a more complex topic than forgiveness. Forgiveness is not a one-time act; it is a process. We can be someone who is horribly confused about what forgiveness is and what it is not and live our lives in bitterness with the real risk of never understanding that we could have lived life differently. For many of you, the reason you are involved in this study is because you are trying to grapple with a very difficult situation in your own life or in the lives of those closest to you.

I will ask many questions of us during this study. The first one I want to ask you is who do you need to forgive and why do you struggle with forgiving him or her? Please be as specific as you can. You will not be asked to share this with anyone.

Ezekiel 36:26 says:
I will give you a new heart and put a new spirit in you; I will remove from you your heart of stone and give you a heart of flesh.

Are we walking around with a heart of stone toward the one who has caused us such pain, my dear sisters? If we have something to forgive someone for, we may have a heart that is fortified and impenetrable. Betrayal, not being protected or defended like we should have been, the death of a life we once knew, and the need for revenge can haunt us daily. What may be hidden from us is the depth to which our own heart is fortified like a fortress. To understand why this is so we need to understand the foundations on which that fortification is built. It is my prayer that we will soon start to see our God answering our cry for help to change our heart of stone into a heart of flesh.

As we end today, use the margin to make Jeremiah 33:3 the prayer of your heart by:

1) Calling out to God and telling Him what you need from Him regarding forgiveness in your heart. Confess the state of your heart toward the one you need to forgive. God knows your hurt anyway, so it will not shock Him. Sometimes we do not know our own hearts. Ask Him to start replacing your heart of stone in this area with a heart of flesh that is receptive to His leading.

2) Thank Him that He is going to answer you.

3) Now give the Lord praise for what He is going to show you that you did not know before.

May God bless us with insight as we call out to the One who will hear and answer us and show us great and unsearchable things that we did not know before!

Day 2 – A Look at Our Family Tree

I don't think I know anyone personally who has clear memories of his or her great-grandparents. I have two friends whose grandparents just passed away within the last year, but I have never met an adult friend whose great grandparent was still alive or whose memories of that person do not come from old photographs contained in an album or staring out of a picture frame.

I have seen one picture of my maternal great-grandmother. The faded black and white photograph shows her on a wrap around porch wearing a sunbonnet. She had four daughters, one of them being my grandmother, Ruth. She died when my mother was a little girl. There are just a handful of facts I know about her. She was a culinary artist with flour, lard and salt. Although she never lived above the poverty level, she could whip up the tastiest food with the smallest amount of ingredients. Her baked goods were legendary in my grandmother's memory. The southern air of Arkansas was where Mamie Leyden drew her first breath as well as her last.

Let's have a little fun here. We are going to fill in our family trees by including our great-grandparents' names, grandparents' names, parents' names, our name, and our child(ren)'s name(s) (if applicable) below. Realizing that some of our family trees are more complicated, I have included spots for significant others (e.g., step-parents or step/half-siblings)

____________________ (Father's grandparents)   ____________________ (Mother's grandparents)

____________________ (Father's parents)   ____________________ (Mother's parents)

____________________ (Father)   ____________________   ____________________ (Mother)

____________________ (sibling)   ____________________ (my name)   ____________________ (sibling)

____________________   ____________________ (my child/ren)   ____________________

____________________   ____________________ (significant others)   ____________________

One sad fact I do know about my great-grandmother is that she lived in tremendous fear. Paralyzed by her own anxiety, she would gather her four little girls to her and fly under the bed whenever a stranger knocked on the door. My grandmother remembers being warned to be quiet until her mother told her and her sisters that the stranger had left. Perhaps if Mamie Leyden had been married to someone who treated her well, my great-grandmother would have been a different person, but her deacon husband had a roving eye. A lack of security in her marriage caused by his infidelity may have played a significant role in the grip of fear that shaped much of her life.

I will admit to you that some of my least favorite chapters in the Bible are the ones that list the genealogies of families. It is a great temptation for me to skip over all the *begats* and *born to so-and-so verses* in Scripture. I believe with all my heart that **all** Scripture is inspired by God and is useful for teaching, rebuking, correcting, and training me in righteousness (2 Timothy 3:16), but I used to be puzzled and never understood why God decided to include verse after verse of obscure family members until I realized that God is all about families. The family dynamic is incredibly important to Him – so important that He even communicates to us about the members of the three Persons who make up the holy Trinity as Father, Son, and Holy Spirit.

What do the following verses tell us about the importance of families? Write a brief sentence or two to summarize each of the following verses:

Families are very important to God. A huge step toward healing is to recognize the flaws and acknowledge that the dysfunction exists in every one of our families.

John 7:42:

Ephesians 3:14-16:

1 Timothy 3:2-5:

Hebrews 2:11:

1 Peter 4:16-17:

Jesus Christ was part of a family line. Our salvation found in Jesus Christ makes us part of God's family – the greatest family ever to exist. Families are very important to God.

I lived many years under the delusion that some families (including mine) were free from dysfunction. My heart would burn with sympathy as friends would share some of their deepest hurts with me over what had taken place in their homes as they grew up. *Why can't they just kiss and make up?* I would ignorantly think in my lack of empathy for their pain. I have come to realize that perfect families only exist on Currier and Ives Christmas cards, not in real life. Wounds and pain exist in families that are far more complex than a simple hug and kiss will mend and change. A huge step toward healing is to recognize the flaws and acknowledge that the dysfunction exists in every one of our families. Each family is made up of sinful, broken people who desperately need a Savior. Until we take off our rose-colored glasses and carefully observe where the source of the dysfunction is and start crying out for deliverance for our families in those areas, we will continue to hurt each other deeply.

Please read 2 Corinthians 10:3-5 and write out verse four here:

I looked up the definition of ***stronghold*** in a number of dictionaries. Most of the definitions included were synonyms for a fortress, garrison or a prison. While strongholds are not always evil in nature, in the verses above the apostle Paul describes them as defensive structures set up by our own sinful nature and Satan's forces to give us false protection from the truth. Our strongholds keep us from true deliverance and freedom. Only divine power given us by the Holy Spirit can demolish these damaging fortifications. Some of the strongholds we encounter in our families are characterized in Colossians 3:5-10. Underline all destructive behaviors you find listed in the following verses:

5 Put to death, therefore, whatever belongs to your earthly nature: sexual
immorality, impurity, lust, evil desires and greed, which is idolatry. 6 Because
of these, the wrath of God is coming. 7 You used to walk in these ways, in the
life you once lived. 8 But now you must rid yourselves of all such things as these:
anger, rage, malice, slander, and filthy language from your lips. 9 Do not lie to
each other, since you have taken off your old self with its practices 10 and have
put on the new self, which is being renewed in knowledge in the image of its Creator.

Our strongholds keep us from true deliverance and freedom.

I want us to go back to our family tree at the beginning of this lesson. Has sexual immorality or lust (including pornography) been a pattern in your family? Did a grandparent or parent have an explosive temper? Was filthy language and taking God's name in vain a part of the everyday language of your household growing up? Do you struggle with using R-rated language in your speech? Has betrayal, lying and deceit been a way of life in your family line? Did your parent, grandparent or great-grandparent live a life of idolatry – worshiping at the shrine of work, money, power, prestige, or an addiction (alcoholism, drug abuse, an eating disorder, etc.) to the detriment of his or her family?

List the underlined sin above and put the first initial of those in your family who have struggled with those sins here:

Perhaps this list of sins do not describe the strongholds represented in your family tree. Maybe the strongholds you see most have to do with an inability to forgive or fear. 2 Timothy 1:7 assures me that my God has not given me a spirit of fear, but one of power, love, and of a sound mind. Fear is all over my family tree on my maternal side. Each of the four generations has struggled because of fear's paralyzing grip. I see signs of the stronghold of fear showing up in my own children. Fear does not come from God. It is a stronghold fortified by the enemy whose goal in our lives is to steal, kill, and destroy us (John 10:10).

Where and how has fear shown up in your family? Include the first initial of these family members names after your answer:

Unforgiveness has been a big problem for me throughout the years. Some people seem to have the ability to not hold grudges and to easily forgive those who have hurt them. I want to be very honest with you. I am not one of those people. I have never struggled so much in my obedience with Christ than to obey Him in this area. I have come to see through doing this family exercise that bearing a grudge and lack of forgiveness did not start with me. Those sins have found their way into each generation on both sides of my family.

How about you? Who in your family tree has struggled with forgiving others? Put the first initial of their names here.

Look up and match the proceeding passages with the correct reference:

We do not have to continue living in the chains of fear and unforgiveness that we may be carrying today.

Psalm 130:4: God is faithful to forgive confessed sin.

Matthew 6:14: God will forgive me if I forgive others.

Matthew 6:15: With God there is forgiveness; He is to be feared.

1 John 1:9: God will not forgive me if I do not forgive others.

I spent eight formative years of my childhood growing up among the Bayanzi tribe in the Democratic Republic of Congo. Before my grandfather shared the gospel of Jesus Christ with these precious people, they tried to appease the spirits of their dead ancestors through demon worship (truly these were demonic spirits). In a desperate search for atonement, the Bayanzi practiced child sacrifice to those spirits in gruesome, wicked ways. Three generations have passed since the awakening among them and if I introduced my wonderful Congolese family members to you today, you would not be able to believe that their parents and grandparents practiced such evil. The Holy Spirit has completely transformed people who were living in the deepest darkness of sin to some of the greatest heroes of the faith I have ever known.

Each of us has a choice today to begin seeking God to help us demolish these destructive strongholds that have been in our families for generations. We do not have to continue living in the chains of fear and unforgiveness that we may be carrying today.

Write out Colossians 3:7-8 in the margin.

Are those sins listed becoming a more distant way of life for us as we steadfastly pursue a relationship with Christ or are we still clinging to them because we feel justified in doing so because of the hurt that has been caused to us? As we finish this lesson, I want to ask us if we are ready to be, perhaps, the first person in our family to not walk in the old life that has been our family legacy for too long. Unforgiveness, fear, and the other destructive behaviors we looked at in this lesson have brought me nothing but misery in the end. The satisfaction I received from practicing them was very short-lived and truly was no satisfaction at all. The bitterness and pain changed my heart to stone as I held on to their poison. I remained captive within these strongholds.

I don't want to live like that anymore. I want victory instead of defeat. I want gladness instead of mourning. I want freedom instead of the prison I once lived in. How about you?

After reading 2 Corinthians 10:4 again, use the space below to pour out your heart to Jesus who can break those generations-old chains and empower you to walk in a way that brings life.

Let's start walking in the abundant life we have been promised!

Day Three – Her Name Was Sarah

I write to connect with women. While I have been informed by men that the subject of jealousy about which I wrote in my first Bible study and the issues of unforgiveness are universal problems for men and women, I do not write for men. It is my great joy and passion to share the power of the Scriptures with women everywhere. Although I have not been back to the Congo for over twenty years, one of my deepest and repeated prayers is to be able to take my husband and children and return to my adopted country. I would love to pour over Scripture with my Congolese sisters-in-Christ one day and witness the truth that the Word of God is life-giving to any culture or language.

The Bible is the final authority on any subject (2 Timothy 3:16-17), but I didn't start making it my final authority until twelve years ago. I had grown up in Sunday school in a Bible-believing church, but through my adolescent years and into my late twenties, those familiar stories became boring and irrelevant to my way of thinking. I felt intimidated around people who were full of biblical knowledge and jealous of those who had found the secret to making the Bible come alive. I longed for that to happen in my life, too, but thought I would never experience the joy of having the Scripture leap off the page right into my own life circumstances.

I felt intimidated around people who were full of biblical knowledge and jealous of those who had found the secret to making the Bible come alive.

My dear friend, I am praying as I write this that Jesus Christ would reveal Himself to you as you have never experienced Him before. I am begging God to show up and undeniably show Himself to us through the story of the life of Joseph. Would you join me in praying that for yourself right now?

Turn to Genesis 23:17-19 and give a brief description of these verses:

My children never knew my maternal grandparents with whom I had been very close growing up. Chase was around five years old, Jordyn was four and Jenna was two when my mom and I, along with my Aunt Gerry, took my kids to the cemetery where my grandparents are buried beneath the same headstone. The leaves were just beginning to drop and the air had a nip of coolness in it as it brushed our cheeks that beautiful fall day. Soon after we arrived, I saw my son picking up leaves and placing them around the ledge of the headstone. Not understanding what he was doing and wanting to teach him to be respectful of the gravesite, I gently chided him. He looked up at me in childish innocence and said, "Mommy, I was making a blanket for them because it's cold today."

I remember looking at the dates of their births and deaths with the dash in between the numbers. That dash represented eight-six years for my grandmother and almost eighty-nine for my grandfather. Those who would come to the cemetery and pass by the headstone would not know what had taken place in those decades of time. They wouldn't know how dear and wonderful those two people had been to their children and grandchildren.

The ancient world did not have a way of photographing faces. Once a great-grandparent had died, the descendants would have to use the

descriptions given by those living to form their own mental picture of what their ancestors had looked like. I can imagine a day when Abraham's descendants would have all come to the cave of Machpelah to hear the oral family history once again so that they would one day be able to pass the information down to the coming generations yet to be born. The stone sitting at the mouth of the cave would have been the only lasting reminder of the years that the deceased had lived.

During this first week of study, we are going to be filling in the family tree of Joseph starting with the three generations that were born before him. Today we are going to study the great-grandmother of the twelve brothers whom we will spend the majority of our time studying in the weeks to come. Introductions in Scripture are very important.

Please read Genesis 11:27-30. Who was Sarai (later known as Sarah) and how does Scripture describe her in verse 30?

The first characteristic that describes Sarai was that she was barren. For those of us who may be currently struggling or have struggled with infertility in the past, do you have empathy for Sarah believing her identity was wrapped up in her barrenness? Have you felt that everything else about you is overshadowed by your inability to become or stay pregnant? If yes, please share here:

What sin did Abram (Abraham) ask Sarai to commit for him in Genesis 12:10-16 and why do you believe he did that?

After reading, Genesis 16:1-6, what rash decision did Sarai make in verse 2 prompted by her barrenness?

God had promised Abram a son with his wife Sarai as the baby's mother before the destructive events of Genesis 16 happened. Eleven years after the promise was made, Sarai became impatient with God's timetable. Sarai, like me so often, couldn't wait any longer and felt she needed to "help" God help her.

What did Sarai do in verse 6?

Before I judge Sarai, I have to reflect on my own life. God has asked me to wait for something He has promised me, too. I, like Sarai, have acted rashly or at least I have been tempted to manipulate the situation to bring an end to the wait.

How does Micah 7:7 speak to your time of waiting?

The events of Genesis 20 will remind us again of Abraham's paralyzing fear which caused him to lie. After reading Genesis 20:1-17, write down any similarities you see between the actions Abraham took here with Genesis 12:10-16.

I remember well mothers who were older than me observing my three preschool-aged children and me in public. With annoyingly nostalgic expressions I could not relate to at the time, they would longingly look at the group of four we made up and say, "Enjoy these years! They grow up so fast!" Their friendly words of encouragement were completely lost on me as I tried to navigate the aisles with a baby on my hip and my two other preschool-aged children in tow beside me. The early years of motherhood were a blur to me of little sleep, mountains of diapers, and clothing which told everyone who looked closely enough what my children had eaten for lunch.

I, like Sarai, have acted rashly or at least I have been tempted to manipulate the situation to bring an end to the wait.

I was in my late twenties and early thirties when my children were born. I cannot imagine having a baby at ninety years old! The beginning of Genesis 21 opens with the joyous birth of a baby boy named Isaac who brought laughter to the heart of his mother, Sarah, who had waited twenty-five years for his arrival. God had done what Sarah and Abraham had tried to manipulate through Hagar with the birth of Ishmael. Their laughter over the sound of the pitter patter of tiny feet and the endearing small voice of their promised baby must have rung out through the night sky as they tucked him into bed.

But a life-altering event with ramifications which continue to this day was about to transpire in Abraham's life. Let's pick up the story and read Genesis 21:8-20.

What reason did Sarah give for her ultimatum in verses 9-10?

What did Abraham do as a result of Sarah's anger in verse 14?

What was Hagar's reaction over her son's plight in vv. 15-16?

Who came to their rescue in vv. 17-20?

What destructive thoughts might Hagar and Ishmael have had toward Abraham and Sarah over being sent away?

Romans 6:23 tells us that the wages of sin is death - perhaps not physical death, but relational death - the sort which results in the death of trust and the separation of loved ones. Sometimes physical death is easier to mourn for than an emotional or relational death.

Look back at your family tree on the first page of Week One, Day 2. After reflecting on Romans 6:23, where do you see the truth of this verse in the relationships you have listed there?

The ultimate goal of forgiveness is reconciliation.

Although God can heal our messes, we sometimes have to continue to live with the consequences of those messes. He always has the power to redeem, but we will still walk away with scars after our encounter with sin. When we do not wait for God's perfect timing and instead try to manipulate a situation because we falsely believe God did not hear us the first time we called out to Him, the consequences of our unbelief can be generations long. Ishmael spent the rest of his life in a single parent home with his mother Hagar. Ishmael became the father of twelve sons who became the ancestors of the Arab people today. Isaac was the child through whom the Jewish nation of Israel descended. Our daily news is full of the unrest that continues between the two sons of Abraham who still are not reconciled millennia after the events we studied today. Sadly, reconciliation can be as elusive in our own families.

Therefore, if anyone is in Christ, he is a new creation; the old has gone, the new has come! All this is from God, who reconciled us to himself through Christ and gave us the ministry of reconciliation: that God was reconciling the world to himself in Christ, not counting men's sins against them. And he has committed to us the message of reconciliation.

2 Corinthians 5:17-19

If you and I have made Jesus Christ the Lord of our lives, we are not the same people we used to be. This new life that we have been given through Jesus Christ can empower us to forgive what others would tell us is not forgivable. The ultimate goal of forgiveness is reconciliation. The question I want to ask ourselves as we end today's lesson is: are we open to being an instrument of reconciliation to the one who has hurt us when we realize that Christ does not count our sins against us? We will come to learn in the next weeks that forgiveness only requires action on the part of one party while reconciliation takes both parties coming together to heal.

Are you and I willing to be one half of the party should God allow reconciliation to happen in our situations? How we answer that question could mean the start of healing on a level we have never experienced in our relationships. I pray that we will carefully go before the Lord with this vital question as we close today's lesson.

Day Four – The New Lady of the House

Yesterday we looked at the fourth generation back from Joseph and his brothers. While Joseph and his siblings did not know their great-grandparents, Abraham and Sarah, we do know that Joseph's grandfather, Isaac, died after Joseph's brothers were born (see Genesis 35:21-29). Although we cannot know for sure, the siblings may have also known their grandmother, Rebekah, before she passed away.

Please read Exodus 34:6-7. How far-reaching are sin's consequences in generations according to these verses? Circle one:

First and second | Third and fourth

Fifth and sixth | One thousand

Why do the consequences of sin last until the third or fourth generation? One explanation is that it is conceivable for three, perhaps four, generations to live in community with each other. There is a certain facial expression that my son, Chase, wears occasionally that reminds me of his Grandpa Lantz who smiles in the very same way. Is that caused by DNA or Chase emulating his grandfather? I don't know. But just as facial features or expressions show up one, two, or even three generations later, it is possible for sins that have gripped previous generations to be passed down to those who follow behind. Many young people today are being raised by grandparents, sometimes even in the place of their biological parents. One can see how grandparents who act as parents for their grandchildren can pass their own fears and propensities to certain sins to their grandchildren or possibly their great-grandchildren if they are in a close relationship with them. Great, great-grandparents are usually long dead by the time the fifth generation is born.

I did not know my great-grandparents who died long before I was born, but I can easily retrieve from my memory bank some memories of my dad's mother who died when I was ten. I have very vivid memories of my mother's parents who died while I was in my twenties. Some of the greatest joys of my childhood were memories made at their home on Pontiac Lake Road.

How would you describe your relationship with your grandparents? What are some of your memories of them?

Shortly after Sarah died, a new woman came into the life of Abraham and his son, Isaac. Let's meet Rebekah in the following passages of Scripture and answer these questions:

How does Scripture introduce us to her in Genesis 24:15-16? How was she related to Abraham?

With whom did Abraham's servant talk regarding the arrangement of marriage between Rebekah and Isaac in verses 29 and 50-51? Circle one:

Rebekah's mother and father

The priest of the town

Her father and brother

American culture boasts of its freedom to choose. A man meets a woman, they begin a relationship, perhaps fall in love, which may or may not lead to marriage. The culture in which I grew up in Congo has no such thing as dating. The idea of a woman marrying a man she had chosen was considered preposterous and rebellious to her father, brothers, and uncles. Romance plays no part in a Congolese union. Marriages are arranged by male relatives who require a significant dowry from the husband-to-be. Although it may sound foreign and distasteful to us, Abraham's servant finding Rebekah this way was actually the way in which couples came together as marriage partners.

American culture boasts of its freedom to choose.

Skip down to verses 66-67. What major event had recently occurred in Isaac's life? Put a check mark next to the correct answer:
___ The rescue of Isaac on Mount Moriah
___ A move by the family to a new region
___ Sarah's death
___ Ishmael's revenge on the family

Now let's read Genesis 26:1-9. What reaction came from Isaac's fear that is strikingly similar to his father's actions in Genesis 12:10-16 and Genesis 20?

How are Sarah and Rebekah both described in Genesis 12:11 and in 26:8?

What else did the two women share in Genesis 11:30 and 25:21?

Let's read Genesis 25:20-28 and learn more about Isaac's wife and the result of his prayer for her concerning her desire to be a mother.

What caused Rebekah's concern during her pregnancy? Circle one:

Complications   Depression   The babies' behavior in the womb

What did the Lord reveal to her about the babies in verse 23?

Imagine you are Rebekah for a moment. Would you have revealed this conversation between you and the Lord to your husband, Isaac? Why or why not?

I was studying this passage of Scripture with other women several years ago when the question I just asked you was asked of the group. I was fascinated to learn that the majority of the class did not believe that Rebekah ever told Isaac about this exchange between her and the Lord.

What does the Lord desire to happen between a married couple according to Mark 10:7-9?

How do you think secrets between spouses affect the Lord's desire for oneness between a husband and wife?

Did/do your parents have secrets in their marriage? How do you think having secrets affected their marriage? If you are married, do you have secrets from your spouse? Why?

Overwhelmingly, the reason the ladies in my Bible study group said they did not believe Rebekah told Isaac was that she ran the risk of looking stupid in front of her husband. They felt that Isaac perhaps would have doubted that Rebekah had heard the Lord correctly or that Isaac might have dismissed her revelation because the Lord had not revealed this information to him. The ladies could empathize with Rebekah about not wanting Isaac to think she was exaggerating.

Overwhelmingly, the reason the ladies in my Bible study group said they did not believe Rebekah told Isaac was that she ran the risk of looking stupid in front of her husband.

Scripture tells on people! After reading Genesis 3:1-6, what was the third reason listed as to why Eve ate the forbidden fruit in verse 6?

It was "desirable for gaining ______________________."

Is it so important for us to look smart to others that we sin? So many times when I examine my motive behind a sin, the Holy Spirit will reveal the destructive, pride-filled desire to look intelligent in front of others. My need to look wise in front of others can quickly send me down a destructive path.

Going back to Genesis 25:24-28, what did the younger brother, Jacob, do to the older, Esau, at the twins' birth?

What does verse 28 reveal about Isaac and Rebekah's relationship to their sons?

What did the brother of Jesus say about favoritism in James 2:8-9?

Favoritism is deadly, my friend. Pure poison.

Favoritism is deadly, my friend. Pure poison. Some of my most painful memories as a child can be traced back to an adult who preferred someone else over me and did not do a careful job of concealing those feelings of favoritism. I clearly remember an elementary teacher who showed blatant favoritism in our classroom. I was not one of her favorites. I also had an adult relative who favored my siblings over me. This was especially apparent at Christmastime in the number and quality of gifts I would receive compared to my sister and brother. I did not feel loved, respected, valued, or close to either my teacher or this family member. The memory of their favoritism can instantly transport me back to that place of hurt even though the events happened over thirty years ago.

As we close this lesson, I want us to spend some time asking ourselves some difficult questions:

Where has favoritism shown up in your family?

Are we guilty of favoring one child over another because we share common interests with that child or enjoy his or her personality more than another daughter's or son's?
How is our favoritism affecting our children's relationships with their sibling(s)?

Favoritism waters the seeds of unforgivingness and causes bitterness to grow in our families. We must be diligent to recognize this and ask for God's help to remove the root of bitterness.

14 ***But Zion said, "The LORD has forsaken me,***
the Lord has forgotten me."
15 ***"Can a mother forget the baby at her breast***
and have no compassion on the child she has borne?
Though she may forget,
I will not forget you!
16 ***See, I have engraved you on the palms of my hands;***
your walls are ever before me.
17 ***Your children hasten back,***
and those who laid you waste depart from you.
18 ***Lift up your eyes and look around;***
all your children gather and come to you.
As surely as I live," declares the LORD,
"you will wear them all as ornaments;
you will put them on, like a bride. ***Isaiah 49:14-18***

Let's ask the Lord to empower us to believe that although a parent or significant adult may have made us feel forsaken because of favoritism, through His Holy Spirit's strength we can stop the ravaging results of its poison in the generations to come in our families. Trust, intimacy and forgiveness will be the fruit of the harvest from the new seeds planted in our lives.

Day Five – Rebekah's Ruse

The goal of this first week of study has been to examine the influence of sinful patterns among generations in families. I love a biblical narrative because I can peek over the shoulder of the people involved in the story line and readily see their shortcomings which can open my blind eyes to my own lapses of judgment. The Holy Spirit speaks deeply to me through the life story of another as He gently convicts me and points out the similarities between my mistakes and the mistakes made by the person(s) I am studying.

I have come to realize something about myself that is difficult to admit because I despise this characteristic in other people: I love being in control of everything. My need to control has even gone so far as to forbid my youngest daughter from expressing her own unique fashion style. I must tell you it was not for an honorable reason like immodesty that I denied her chosen outfit. I just didn't want others to see the brown shirt with the blue, green, and purple short combination that her four-year-old mind thought looked dazzling. Afterward, what would others think about *me* if they saw her looking like that in public?

Sigh.

The Holy Spirit speaks deeply to me through the life story of another as He gently convicts me and points out the similarities between my mistakes and the mistakes made by the person(s) I am studying.

Rate your need for control by answering the following questions by marking with an X on the following continuums:

In my marriage/relationship with my boyfriend/fiance:

1	5	10
I do not struggle with control issues.	I sometimes struggle with wanting to take control.	This is a huge issue of struggle for me.

With my children and/or parents:

1	5	10
I do not struggle with control issues.	I sometimes struggle with wanting to take control.	This is a huge issue of struggle for me.

With my friends/co-workers:

1	5	10
I do not struggle with control issues.	I sometimes struggle with wanting to take control.	This is a huge issue of struggle for me.

Looking back over your family tree, where have you seen the need for control or manipulation wreak havoc in relationships (e.g. between parents, grandparents, siblings)? How did that manifest itself (e.g. divorce, lack of respect, constant fighting for dominant position, estrangement, etc.)?

Today's lesson is going to focus on the subject of persons wanting to be in control. We have several sections of Scripture to read today. Let's start by reading where we left off yesterday, picking up the story of Isaac and Rebekah's twin sons, Esau and Jacob, in Genesis 25:29-34.

What did Esau want in this passage?

What did Jacob want in this passage (verse 31)? Circle one:

Esau's bow   Esau's birthright   Esau's tent   Esau's stew

Ancient biblical culture placed a significant importance on the birthright of the eldest son that we can easily miss because we are unfamiliar with what the birthright represented. A birthright allowed the oldest son to receive a double portion of the father's estate. The son who received the blessing of the birthright was recognized as the spiritual leader of the extended family after his father's death.

A birthright allowed the oldest son to receive a double portion of the father's estate. The son who received the blessing of the birthright was recognized as the spiritual leader of the extended family after his father's death.

What was Esau's attitude toward the demand Jacob made of him in verses 32, 34? Circle one:

Apathy   Anger   Surprise   Indignation

This was Esau's attitude, but what deeper motive does Scripture reveal regarding Esau's heart in verse 34?

Let's now read Genesis 27:1-13 and answer the following questions:

How did Rebekah specifically speak of her sons in verses 6 (Esau) and 8 (Jacob) that may reveal her feelings of favoritism?

What actions can we see in verses 14-17 which show that Jacob and Rebekah deliberately set out to deceive Isaac?

How many times did Jacob lie to Isaac in verses 18-25?

What convinced Isaac that Jacob's lies were the truth and what were the specific ways Isaac blessed Jacob in verses 27-29? List the blessings in the margin.

Continue reading Genesis 27:30-45.

What did Esau want Isaac to do and what was his reaction to Isaac's answer to his request (verses 30-38)?

What was the end result of Rebekah and Jacob's scheming (verses 41-45)? At what cost did they get what they wanted?

How do you think Rebekah and Jacob's scheme affected...

Isaac and Jacob's relationship?

Isaac and Esau's relationship?

Isaac and Rebekah's relationship?

Esau and Rebekah's relationship?

Rebekah and Jacob's relationship?

Esau and Jacob's relationship?

We have a tendency to doubt the absolute trustworthiness of God.

Hebrews 12:15 says: *See to it that no one falls short of the grace of God and that no bitter root grows up to cause trouble and defile many.* Sin never defiles just one person. We cannot keep sin contained as hard as we might try. Our sin has far-reaching and devastating consequences when it goes unconfessed and we remain unrepentant.

God had told Abraham that He would give him a son; however God did not reveal when. Sarah decided she would help God out and willingly gave another woman into her husband's arms. The consequences of that rash decision forced the disfavored son, Ishmael, to live away from his father for all of his adult life.

We have a tendency to doubt the absolute trustworthiness of God. Although we might never call Him a liar, when we do not get what we want when we want it, we can start to behave in ways that reveal our lack of faith in His promises to us. Isaac and Rebekah sowed a bitter crop in their family because of the sin of their favoritism toward their sons.

I have often thought back to a conversation my husband and I had about our children when they were preschoolers. He made a profound observation. As we were watching them play, he said of our three, "They are programmed to love us and need us to love them back."

We can achieve amazing accomplishments and continue chasing after our parents' approval if their favoritism has set us up against our own siblings to compete for their love. Grown men and women still long to hear, "I am so proud of you, son." Or "I dreamed of having a daughter just like you."

Have you received your parents' approval? How has their approval or lack of approval affected you in:

1) your motivation to achieve:

2) your confidence in your talents/giftings:

3) your trust that God accepts you:

If you are a parent, do each of your children know that they have your approval? When was the last time you told each one you delighted in and loved him/her even if that child is not the easiest to get along with or has disappointed you in some way?

Rebekah was specifically told by the Lord that the younger of her twins would serve the older one. God's timing is everything! Tragically, Rebekah fell into the trap that I so often fall into when I grasp for control of a situation instead of letting God work things out. I overlook that He does not need my help! The Creator of the universe, the One who has the power to work all things to conform to His will, has a plan that will allow me to escape the tainting of sin when I let Him have control of my life. I do not need to jockey for position. He will take care of everything ... in His own timing. And that is what is so difficult to wait for.

The Creator of the universe, the One who has the power to work all things to conform to His will, has a plan that will allow me to escape the tainting of sin when I let Him have control of my life.

Rebekah chose not to believe God at His Word. She pitted her husband against her favorite son which resulted in distrust between Isaac and Jacob. A consequence of her attempt to control caused Esau to want to murder his brother. Esau's murderous rage led to Rebekah suffering a devastating separation from Jacob, who would not return for twenty years after he fled from home to escape Esau's wrath. Scripture never records a reunion between Rebekah and Jacob. Perhaps they never saw one another again. My dear friend, manipulation will always get us into trouble and may perhaps be the very reason we lose what we hold most dear.

Where are you and I jockeying for position in our families? Look back at your family tree (page 6) and write ***control*** where manipulation has shown its ugly face among family members.

But the Lord's plans stand firm forever; his intentions can never be shaken.
Psalm 33:11 (NLT)

Do we believe that our God has a way to bring about those plans that will stand firm forever? Do we not believe His character and think we need to help Him help us or someone else? If we believe that Psalm 33:11 is the truth, we do not have to manipulate or try to control others! We will avoid many problems and much evil if we believe that God is big enough to handle any scheme of man or the enemy to rob us of what He has willed.

This week has not been an easy one, dear friend! I am so proud of your tenacity and your willingness to uncover the poison that has been either glaringly evident or hiding beneath the surface of our most important relationships. I heard this on Christian radio this week:

There is no such thing as failure when we have a Redeemer with the power to change our failures into new beginnings. – Chip Ingram

Your family tree may look like one big failure loaded down with the sins of three or four generations. Please do not be discouraged as the enemy, Satan would want us to be. We are a people of hope because we trust in the One who has the power to heal what has been broken for so long. With that perspective, let's hand over what we cannot control anyway and bow our knee to the Almighty God who will work miracles in our lives if we are willing to let Him.

A House Divided

The year was 1858 and a towering figure stood to deliver a speech in the Hall of Representatives in Springfield, Illinois. The man hoping to be selected as the the Republican candidate for the U.S. Senate did not have the support of his law partner for his decision to use the following words of Christ as part of his speech:

If a house is divided against itself, that house cannot stand.
– Mark 3:25

The law partner warned the political hopeful that using these words of Christ to describe the mounting tension dividing the union of the United States over the issue of slavery were fundamentally true, but politically incorrect. In response to his friend's caution, the statesman replied:

"The proposition is indisputably true ... and I will deliver it as written. I want to use some universally known figure, expressed in simple language as universally known, that it may strike home to the minds of men in order to rouse them to the peril of the times." [1]

Unfortunately, Abraham Lincoln was correct. He went on to become the sixteenth president of a divided nation ripped apart over the issue of slavery. A bloody civil war ensued, lasting four long years.

This week of study we will examine the ravaging effects of deceit and jealousy in the lives of the four women who called themselves the wives of Jacob. We will see the ugly faces of sibling rivalry and jealousy drive two sisters to make desperate decisions as each contributed in building a divided home.

Look closely, my friend! We must not let the Word of God remain only words on a page. We must ask ourselves if our own homes are being divided by jealousy caused by favoritism and the lack of forgiveness.

May the warning strike home to our minds and rouse us to the peril of a house divided.

Day One – A Sad Escape and an Unexpected Encounter

I used to think that the Old Testament was full of archaic stories that were so far-removed from my life and culture that I could not possibly relate to the main characters involved in them. How wrong I was! The deeper we dig in this study, the more we will realize there are some basic needs we all have as human beings that will never change, my dear friend. People will always want to be respected, loved, and treated well. When people feel that they are being disrespected, are not loved, and are treated poorly, the relationships in which they are involved become chaotic. Although we will be looking at family relationships that happened thousands of years ago, I suspect that Jacob's family will share striking similarities to our own at times.

People will always want to be respected, loved, and treated well. When people feel that they are being disrespected, are not loved, and are treated poorly, the relationships in which they are involved become chaotic.

Let's remind ourselves of where we left off last week by reading Genesis 27:41-46 and matching the following names with the correct sentence:

Rebekah	Held a grudge and wanted to kill his brother.
Isaac	Rebekah's brother who lived in a distant land.
Jacob	Was told to flee for his life and stay away for a time.
Esau	Was informed of his wife's disgust over the wives of Esau.
Haran	Warned Jacob to leave home until Esau forgot.
Laban	A distant land requiring days of travel.

Wanting the companionship of other children my age, I attended boarding school in seventh grade six hundred miles away from home. A dense jungle separated me from our mission station. The distance was only traversed by a four hour airplane ride. The mission school that I attended was home to about forty children from second to twelfth grade. Saturday mornings were spent doing our assigned chores and perhaps having enough time after their completion to make a trip to the local marche (market) on the mission station. After buying salted peanuts from the market, my favorite activity during a lazy Saturday afternoon was to lie in my bed, stuffing peanuts in my mouth, while devouring a Nancy Drew book. I relished living vicariously through Nancy Drew as she solved another mystery with her quick thinking and cleverness. By the end of the book, she had not only caught the bad guys, but had uncovered their motives as well.

Life's problems are never wrapped up as neatly as they are in a fictional 250 page book. Our lives can be ones of intense complexity in which we can look in vain for answers. We can be painfully blind to what may be hidden in plain sight because we are so close to the conflict. None of us acts out of a vacuum. We react to a situation in a certain way for a reason. Our past is always part of our present and our future actions. But when painful events happen to us in our families, we can be so close to the hurt that we cannot discern what someone else may be able to who is more objective and removed from our lives. We will read horrific events in Scripture in the next seven weeks and wonder how certain individuals could be so blind to their conduct. Isn't it ironic that we can be so blind to our own?

After reading Genesis 28:1-9, what was the reason Isaac gave for sending Jacob away according to vv. 1-2? Circle one.

Isaac was angry.

Isaac wanted Jacob to find a wife.

Isaac was afraid of Esau.

Place a check beside the statement that best describes how your family dealt with conflict:

_______ We avoided conflict like the plague by never talking about our feelings.

_______ We screamed and called each other names, got angry, didn't apologize to each other, and never mentioned the incident again.

_______ We got upset with each other, but we generally resolve(d) our issues in a way that included forgiveness, respect, and love for the other person.

Do you continue to deal with conflict in the same way now with others? Explain:

How did Esau deal with the fact that Jacob had deceived Isaac for the blessing inteded for him in verses 6-9?

____

Looking back at Genesis 27:41-45, who talked to whom about what had happened?

Esau talked to ____.

Rebekah talked to ____________________________________.

Isaac talked to ______________________________________.

Have you ever been caught up in a family situation where everyone is talking about the problem you have with another family member except for you and the family member with whom you have the problem? If yes, did that help or hurt the resolution of the problem? Share your experience:

____

____

____

God will not remove the consequences when we sin to manipulate a situation in our favor!

By the time we are adults, behaviors we learned in childhood and adolescence usually follow us into our interactions with others. All four people in this family (parents and children) were adults. Although Scripture is silent, we can infer that deception and avoidance were a "normal" way of dealing with conflict in the family of Isaac and Rebekah and their sons. Habits die hard. Scripture gives us no word on whether Isaac brought his sons together to encourage the brothers to forgive each other. Neither are we led to believe that Isaac confronted Rebekah over her scheming with Jacob to deceive him and steal Esau's first-born blessing. Instead, the family was ripped apart by the wound of deception with one another and avoidance of forgiveness and reconciliation.

Rebekah had gone to God with questions over the babies jostling in her womb before her sons were ever born. What did God reveal to Rebekah about Jacob's position of authority over his brother in Genesis 25:23? What does Rebekah's deception toward her husband and Esau reveal about her belief in God's ability to fulfill His plan for her sons?

What does Proverbs 21:30 reassure us?

There is no _________, no insight, no ________ that can

_________ against the LORD.

My dear friend, what might you and I be fretting over and scheming to get that will cause disunity and heartbreak for others, including ourselves? God will not remove the consequences when we sin to manipulate a situation in our favor! We can honestly think our scheme worked and be left with devastation in our relationships that may take years on this earth or heaven to heal. Is what we want really worth that? Do we truly understand that God has means and methods to accomplish His will for our lives that transcend our understanding? Moreover, when God performs His work in our lives what is brought about is done thoroughly, completely, and promote the abundant life He promised us.

How did each brother react to the conflict that was unresolved between them?

Jacob (Genisis 28:5)

Esau (Genesis 28:8-9)

Let's continue by reading Genesis 28:10-22.

During the physically demanding days of raising my three preschoolers, I often wished I could split myself down the middle to allow myself to be in more than one place at a time. One day, without me realizing her absence, my youngest daughter left me to go get a glass out of the cupboard because she was thirsty. Instead of telling me about her thirst, Jenna decided to climb up onto the counter to reach the cupboard where the glasses were. Suddenly I heard from the other room the sound of shattering glass and Jenna's scream. I rushed into the kitchen hoping I would not see blood everywhere. There was no blood, but my three-year-old, surrounded by hundreds of shards of broken glass, looked up at me with tears in her eyes and whispered, "Momma, can we glue it?"

"No, honey," I replied, "We are going to have to throw this one away."

As Jacob lay down to sleep with a rock for his pillow, I have to wonder what he might have thought about as he pondered all that had brought him to that place between Beersheba and Haran. Shattered glass is trivial and usually replacable. Shattered relationships are neither trivial nor easily put back together.

Shattered glass is trivial and usually replacable. Shattered relationships are neither trivial nor easily put back together.

Glancing over the passage we just read, who came to Jacob the first night away from the home he had always known and how did the person come?

Isaac   Abimelech   The LORD   Jacob's servant

In the margin, record the seven promises he made to Jacob in verses 13-15.

Compare these verses to Genesis 17:1-2 and Genesis 26:3-5. Who were these promises directed to and who made the promises?

After reading vv. 16-22, record Jacob's response to God's offer:

Have you ever been told by someone in a position of honor or authority above you that he or she would like to bless you with something you did not feel you were worthy of? If you have an example of this, please share here:

God Himself had met Jacob on one of the loneliest nights of his life. Jacob knew, unmistakably that his dream was no ordinary one. Jacob, whose name meant schemer, trickster, swindler, was overwhelmed at God's offer to never leave him, to provide for his every need, and to bring Jacob back to the home that he had been forced to leave. In a faltering attempt to accept God's graciousness, Jacob took the rock pillow he had laid on and turned it into a memorial stone.

Underline everything you and I are promised as believers in Jesus Christ in Ephesians 1:3-6 below:

You and I have been visited by our God, too, in His revealed Word.

Praise be to the God and Father of our Lord Jesus Christ, who has blessed us in the heavenly realms with every spiritual blessing in Christ. For he chose us in him before the creation of the world to be holy and blameless in his sight. In love he predestined us for adoption to sonship through Jesus Christ, in accordance with his pleasure and will — to the praise of his glorious grace, which he has freely given us in the One he loves.

How would you describe your own level of commitment to the Lord right now? Why?

You and I have been visited by our God, too, in His revealed Word. The four verses above contain His promises to us. But my question to us today is do we believe Him or are we still struggling to make Him fully our God? How we answer that question will determine our future, our family, and the health of the relationships that we are involved in. Watch carefully, my dear friend, as we will see how dangerously complicated and full of strife life can become when we cannot fully embrace the truth of God wanting to be our God through Jacob's eyes this week.

Day Two – Here Comes the Bride(s)!

I remember trying to explain the concept of American dating to a close Congolese friend of mine. I might as well have been trying to explain the complexity of the universe to him because the idea of dating was completely foreign in his culture. There is no such thing as boy meets girl, boy is attracted to girl, boy asks girl out, and eventually proposes to her in the Congo. All marriages are pre-arranged between the young lady's uncles and father and the groom-to-be. The couple has usually known each other or family members all of their lives. Instead of being judged for her physical attractiveness, a young lady is evaluated on whether she will be submissive, a good mother, and an organized keeper of the home. A bridal price based on the woman's excellence in those areas is agreed upon, paid to the uncles and father of the bride and the couple is free to set up their own home. Love comes later, if it comes at all. Divorce is extremely rare and certainly is not a valid reason of the dissolution of the marriage just because the couple has ceased to have romantic feelings for each other.

There is no such thing as boy meets girl, boy is attracted to girl, boy asks girl out, and eventually proposes to her in the Congo.

Rebekah told Isaac Jacob should leave their home because of what reason according to Genesis 27:46?

Actually, Rebekah knew that Esau planned to do what according to Genesis 27:42?

Jacob was forced to leave his family behind because of the murderous intentions of his brother, Esau. Jacob was confronted with the reality that he was all alone. Esau had been married four times over but Jacob was a bachelor. Like many dysfunctional families, not a word was mentioned about Esau's intentions toward Jacob. A more palatable excuse was made for their younger son's departure from the family tent: It was suddenly urgent that Jacob find a wife! The reality of his solitude must have given him added incentive to follow his parents' instructions to find his bride in the new home he would soon have in Paddan Aram.

Let's read Genesis 29:1-14 and answer the following questions:

Where did Jacob stop when he arrived at his destination? Circle one:

A well A tent A river A stable

With whom did he have a conversation at the well and what did they tell him (vv. 3-6)?

Who came along while they were talking and what did Jacob do for her in verse 10?

How romantic! Doesn't it make your heart swoon? Maybe the thought of a stranger watering your sheep doesn't thrill you, but remember, this was in the heat of the day and Jacob had just helped Rachel immensely. An act of chivalry can go a long way to catch the eye of a woman – especially when the act of kindness makes her life easier in some way. Candlelight and flowers are overrated! I swoon when my husband empties the dishwasher for me without me having to ask!

Let's have some fun...please share an act of kindness done by your boyfriend or husband before you were a couple that made you notice him:

We are not told anything about Rachel's emotional response to Jacob, but what was his reaction to meeting her for the first time? Check one:

_____ He told Rachel about Esau and why he had left at home.

_____ He kissed her, started crying, and told her that he was her father's relative.

_____ He took her staff and offered to walk her flock of sheep home.

After reading vv. 13-14, list Laban's reactions to Jacob that would make Jacob feel welcomed and accepted in Laban's home:

Let's read Genesis 29:15-29.

What bargain did Laban and Jacob strike and why?

List the attributes of each of Laban's daughters in verses 16-17:

Leah	Rachel

Write the words of Jacob's request to Laban in verse 21:

"Give me ______ __________________."

Which sister was Jacob requesting (verse 18) and why do you think he had reason to believe that Laban knew whom he was talking about in verse 21?

What did Jacob discover the morning after the wedding night (vs. 25) and what excuse did Laban give for his actions (vv. 26-27)?

One of the most frustrating relationships I have ever been involved in was with someone who ignored what was obvious to suit her needs or whims. We could have an in-depth conversation about something, but if I was not specific down to the last detail, she would give me what I did not ask for and then pretend to act out of ignorance. Jacob had met his match in Laban. The deceiver had been deceived and found himself in a love triangle he had neither wanted nor could escape. How complicated relationships can become when in-laws become outlaws in someone's life.

The Bible speaks of the concept of sowing and harvesting in our lives. Match the following verses to the correct reference:

A person will reap what she sows.	James 3:18
Those who sow trouble reap it.	Galatians 6:7-8
Peacemakers who sow in peace reap a harvest of righteousness.	Job 4:8

What do you and I do when our expectations collide with our reality? Jacob had worked seven long years for Rachel. He had not complained about the work. He had been faithful to fulfill his obligations, but the one who had schemed his way through life now found the harvest he was reaping was not what he had wanted. Trouble with a capital "T" was just around the corner.

What attribute does Romans 16:27 give to God?

More than seven years had passed since Jacob had communed with God in a way important enough to be recorded in the pages of Scripture. God had not revoked His promise to Jacob to be His God. He had not moved away from Jacob, but we are not given reason to believe that Jacob had moved towards God. When we think we can do things on our own without consulting our God who is the source of all wisdom, we can fool ourselves into thinking that we have a situation under control.

What is the two word directive Paul gives us in 1 Thessalonians 5:17?

______________________ ____________________________

When have you realized that you mistakenly thought you were in control and did not pray through the situation? What was the outcome?

The apostle Paul also continually asked God to fill the church at Colosse with the knowledge of His will through all the wisdom and understanding that the Spirit gives (Colossians 1:9). We desperately need the wisdom of God in all that concerns us, but especially in the area of relationships. My husband, Rob, and I have talked about how little we knew about each other when we got married. I stand amazed at the graciousness of God to us when I consider how seldom I prayed for the character of my future mate. I prayed a great deal to find a mate, but I did not pray that he would love Jesus with all of his heart, soul, and mind. Looking back, I could have made a decision with life-long consequences that would have been difficult to live with. Before I was born, my parents started praying that God would provide a faithful and godly husband for me. I am forever indebted that they stood in the gap for me when I was not mature enough to do that for myself. My dear friend, we are to pray continually, without ceasing. Our own wisdom will get us into trouble every time. We, like Jacob, can be blinded by someone's handsome or beautiful face, charming personality, smooth talk, or fraudulent spirituality. Without prayer, we could be walking into a trap with life-long implications.

We desperately need the wisdom of God in all that concerns us, but especially in the area of relationships.

Our God is the God of today! We can start praying now, even if we have never really prayed about the relationships in our lives. Whether we are in a relationship in which we are inextricably involved and cannot get out without sinning against God or we are in relationships which we have a choice to be involved in, both need unceasing prayer.

Are there any relationships that you need to start praying for continually? What is the Holy Spirit prompting you to pray for in each of the following relationships (if applicable)?

Parent(s):

Sibling(s):

Boyfriend/Husband:

Children:

Friend(s):

Employer/Employee:

Co-worker:

I wanted to end this day of study by letting you, my friend, know what I have asked God for on your behalf as you meet with Him in the pages of His Word:

I keep asking that the God of our Lord Jesus Christ, the glorious Father, may give you the Spirit of wisdom and revelation, so that you may know him better. I pray that the eyes of your heart may be enlightened in order that you may know the hope to which he has called you, the riches of his glorious inheritance in his holy people, and his incomparably great power for us who believe...

Ephesians 1:17-19

May your time in His Word be life-changing and enlightening in a way that can only be experienced by those who take Him up on His promise to show them great and unsearchable things that they do not know by calling out to Him. I want that so desperately in my life and relationships. That is my heart's desire for you!

Day Three – A Tale of Two Sisters

I was once in a dating relationship which stripped me of my dignity and self-worth. *Desperate* would be a good word to describe what I was willing to put up with to keep this person in my life. The fear of being alone was worse than the wandering that was happening to me emotionally and spiritually because of my entanglement with him. I should have been furious with him when I found out that he had started to see someone else while still pretending to be interested in me. Instead, my anger went toward the young woman who became my rival for his affections. I had convinced myself that any time with him was better than none, even if I had to eat the crumbs. By the time I finally walked away from the destruction, I was broken in ways that took years to heal. I pray that my own two daughters will never feel that they must share a man with another woman.

I enjoyed a very close relationship with my sister growing up. She and I lived through some very difficult years together away from our family at boarding school. Hard times have a way of bonding two people together and that was what happened betweeen us. I never felt competitive with Nicol. We were happy for the other when something wonderful happened and sad for the other when something bad happened to the other.

Unfortunately, for many siblings, this is not the case. Some of the worst rivalries experienced have happened between siblings. Today's reading in Genesis is going to show us how nasty and complex a relationship can become between two women whose DNA originates from the same mother and father.

I would like us to include some of yesterday's reading today. What we learn today about the wives of Jacob will serve as important foundational information we will need to understand for later events we will see in the life of Joseph and his brothers.

I had convinced myself that any time with him was better than none, even if I had to eat the crumbs.

Let's read Genesis 29:16-30 and reflect on the two sister-brides of Jacob: Leah and Rachel. Write your insights to the questions below about the appropriate sister under her name (their names appear on the next page):

What was the birth order of the two sisters?
What physical attribute(s) did each have? What attribute(s) would you rather have describe you?
Which sister was Jacob willing to work for to marry? For how long?
What was each sister's expectation toward Jacob at the end of that time (think on this one!)?
Which sister shared the first wedding night with Jacob? Who was responsible for that (vv. 22-23)?
Describe how Leah and Rachel may each have felt about their father's scheming.
What did Laban give to each daughter as a gift (vv. 24, 29)?
What was Jacob's reaction to his bride the following morning? What did he do?
What did Laban do in verse 28?

Which sister was loved by Jacob according to verse 30?

<u>Leah</u> <u>Rachel</u>

What insight does Ecclesiastes 4:4 give to explain people's behavior? Write the verse out here:

Looking over your two lists comparing the sisters, I would like you to now include your observation of where envy might be lurking within the verses we have just read.

Looking over one sister's envy might be easier to uncover, but I believe the other sister had reasons to be envious also. Write those down at the end of the above lists and discuss them in your group.

It is invaluable to be in community with other believers who want to study God's Word.

I would love to hear your answers! There is something so wonderful about discussing Scripture with someone else. He or she may see have a different approach to the same Scripture than I do because of life experiences that differ from mine. It is invaluable to be in community with other believers who want to study God's Word.

Write a brief sentence stating what the following verses reveal about the danger of envy:

Job 5:2:

Proverbs 14:30:

Galatians 5:26:

James 3:16:

Jealousy is a cancer, my dear friend – even when we think that jealousy is justified. This study is devoted to uncovering what biblical forgiveness looks like. I believe that we, as Christian women, are hardly more confused by a subject than this one. Jealousy and unforgiveness tend to walk together hand-in-hand. Those two sins left unredeemed by the blood of Jesus will cause us to do acts of unspeakable harm to one another. The deeper we dig into God's magnificent Word, the more we will see the horror and dysfunction caused by unresolved issues of jealousy and unforgiveness in the family of Jacob.

Looking back at your family tree in week one, where has jealousy and unforgiveness caused devastation? Is there someone in your family who has been excluded from family functions/reunions because of an unresolved conflict? Are there empty chairs representing family members not present at holiday celebrations because the mere mention of their names causes the air to be filled with tension?

What does John 10:10 reveal as Satan's mission as a thief in our lives? Circle one.

To steal, kill, and destroy To make us fearful
To make us doubt God

Has Satan been allowed to carry out his mission in our own family's lives? How?

I believe the purpose of why Satan sets out to steal, kill, and destroy is found in Psalm 145:3-5 (NKJV):

Great is the LORD, and greatly to be praised;
And His greatness is unsearchable.

One generation shall praise Your works to another,
And shall declare Your mighty acts.

I will meditate on the glorious splendor of Your majesty,
And on Your wondrous works.

Instead of giving honor and glory to the Lord, the jealous heart is consumed with the need to be noticed, to be significant, to be loved, and looks to human beings instead of to the Lord to fill those needs.

Satan does not want God's love and praise to pass from one generation to the next. He wants to destroy our families with bitterness and hatred.Self-absorption is the basis of jealousy and unforgiveness. The jealous heart struggles with four core heart issues:

God, can I trust You? God, do You love me? God, are You good? God, are You just?

The object of our jealousy is often the object of our unforgiveness. Our jealous behavior can cause us to behave in ways in which the other person may struggle to forgive us for. Instead of giving honor and glory to the Lord, the jealous heart is consumed with the need to be noticed, to be significant, to be loved, and looks to human beings instead of to the Lord to fill those needs.

The Old Testament book of Judges brings to life the frightening result of what happened when the nation of Israel became jealous of other nations' false gods and ceased worshiping Jehovah, the true God:

After that whole generation had been gathered to their ancestors, another generation grew up who knew neither the LORD nor what he had done for Israel.
Judges 2:10

Has Satan infiltrated our families so that we no longer have unity and do not proclaim as a unit the great acts that God has done for us to our children? Will our own children be able to point to acts of forgiveness in the life of their mother which reveals to them her own deliberate decision to break the chains and devastation of jealousy and unforgiveness in her family? If we dig our heels in and continue to nurse and fester wounds caused years ago, our own children may have very little desire to continue following the Lord in their own families.

What has Satan stolen, killed, and/or destroyed in your family due to jealousy and unforgiveness?

The psalmist talks about meditating in Psalm 145:5 on the glorious splendor and majesty of our God. Instead of meditating on why we have the right to continue harboring bitter envy and selfish ambition in our hearts because of what he or she did to us, we can meditate on the rescue plan that Jesus Christ has said is ours to free us from those heavy chains:

The Spirit of the Sovereign LORD is on me,
because the LORD has anointed me
to proclaim good news to the poor.
He has sent me to bind up the brokenhearted,
to proclaim freedom for the captives
and release from darkness for the prisoners,
2 ***to proclaim the year of the LORD's favor***
and the day of vengeance of our God,
to comfort all who mourn,
3 ***and provide for those who grieve in Zion —***
to bestow on them a crown of beauty
instead of ashes,
the oil of joy
instead of mourning,
and a garment of praise
instead of a spirit of despair.
They will be called oaks of righteousness,
a planting of the LORD
for the display of his splendor.
4 ***They will rebuild the ancient ruins***
and restore the places long devastated;
they will renew the ruined cities
that have been devastated for generations.
Isaiah 61:1-4

The enemy is thwarted in his evil schemes against us and our children when we willingly make the costly decision to allow God to release us from jealous and unforgiving patterns.

The enemy is thwarted in his evil schemes against us and our children when we willingly make the costly decision to allow God to release us from jealous and unforgiving patterns. Hallelujah that our Jesus is the Rebuilder of our devastation!

Day Four – Playing the Fool

Broken hearts ... Loveless marriages ... Divorce ... Strained/abusive relationships between parents and children ... Funerals.

God never intended for us to experience the brokeness that comes from these wounds. Never. These wounds are all part of the deadly consequences of sin to relationships either by ourselves or those close to us. When the Godhead created human beings in their own glorious Image (Genesis 1:26-27), death of relationships and of our physical bodies did not exist. The three holy Persons of the trinity, Father, Son, and Holy Spirit, were perfect and in complete fellowship with each other. Adam and Eve were created in perfection with the intention of their Creator for them to know and worship Him alone and to never experience separation from God, each other, or from those they loved.

What do the following passages reveal about sin? Summarize with a sentence:

Isaiah 59:1-2:

Jeremiah 5:24-25:

Daniel 9:5:

Romans 6:23:

What did David cry out to God in Psalm 13:1? Circle one:

Vengeance toward his enemies   God had forgotten him

About David's anger

The most foolish, regrettable decisions I made in my life came from the desperate need I had to satisfy my longing to be loved by someone.

One of the most devastating consequences of sin is the lie we can believe that our God has abandoned us. We look to another human being to fill the void in our souls that belongs to God alone. The most foolish, regrettable decisions I made in my life came from the desperate need I had to satisfy my longing to be loved by someone. When my heart was broken with the realization that another human being could not fulfill that ache in my soul and I was left with the guilt of my decisions, I, like David, believed the lie that God was against me, and that He had abandoned me in the mess my life had become.

I am praying that the passage that we read today would be seen through new eyes. Growing up with parents who read to their children from the Scriptures, I know I have heard the verses of Genesis many times before. But only after I cried out to God to open His Word to me in a fresh way as an adult have I been able to see these familiar stories with the power that comes from having the Holy Spirit as my Teacher. I pray that He alone would guide this

lesson and empower us to see ourselves in the actions we are going to study of two sisters who had to live with the impossible challenge – having the same man as their husband.

After reading Genesis 29:31, what part did the Lord play toward each sister? This verse clearly indicates that the Lord had control over each sister's ability to conceive. Does that shock you to realize this truth when we live in a world of high tech medical intervention?

Have you ever experienced infertility, miscarriage, or the loss of a baby? Use three words to describe how you felt as you suffered through that time?

I agonized over my first pregnancy ending in a miscarriage. I despised every pregnant woman I met or saw. I would relive my grief and compare my failure with her success in having children. That time was one of the most miserable seasons of my life, aggravated by the fact that I did not have the assurance that I would ever become a mother. I have someone close to me that has not only lost a child, but has experienced three miscarriages following her child's death. Her grief has been unimaginable as she has suffered through this season of life with empty arms that ache to hold a baby of her own in them again. Infertility can make us women feel so inept, so without value, like such failures.

Infertility can make us women feel so inept, so without value, like such failures.

I want to ask this next question as tenderly as I possibly can. I stand as one of you who struggled so much in this area after the loss of my first pregnancy. I did not understand or, frankly, want to submit to the truth that the Lord was the One who controlled my ability to conceive. I did not want to relinquish control. I was angry and bitter and obsessed with nothing else. My obsession to become a mother drove my days and robbed me of many nights' sleep. Instead of pouring out my hurt to the Lord, I spent more money than I can count over pregnancy tests. I did not live in the present. I lived in the future – a future that I wanted more than anything else, but never knew for sure would be mine. Each month my hope was shattered, my hurt became deeper. I did not trust God to be in control of my womb because I could not bear the thought that He may never give me what I wanted. I did not seek His face.

Do you and I understand that God Himself enables us to conceive and carry a baby? And after that baby is born, do we understand that He alone is able to sustain life? Or are we looking to science for answers and the security we want most desperately? Why are we struggling with trusting God in this area? Please share honestly here.

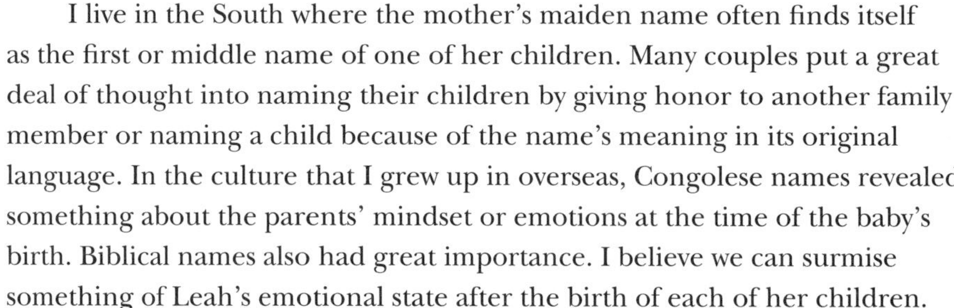

I live in the South where the mother's maiden name often finds itself as the first or middle name of one of her children. Many couples put a great deal of thought into naming their children by giving honor to another family member or naming a child because of the name's meaning in its original language. In the culture that I grew up in overseas, Congolese names revealed something about the parents' mindset or emotions at the time of the baby's birth. Biblical names also had great importance. I believe we can surmise something of Leah's emotional state after the birth of each of her children.

After reading Genesis 29:32-35 write the meanings of the names of each of Leah's four sons and her emotional state attached to each of the names she gave them:

Son's name and its meaning	Leah's mindset
1)	
2)	
3)	
4)	

What differentiated the meaning of Judah from the other three names?

He who sacrifices thank offerings honors me, and he prepares the way so that I may show him the salvation of God. ***Psalm 50:23***

What does a sacrifice of praise do for us, my sweet sister? According to the above verse, praising God when we do not feel like doing so actually prepares the way so that we may see His salvation in our circumstances! How do we start moving forward in spite of our pain? We praise Him. When we finally realize that no human being is going to love us unconditionally and we praise our Jesus that He is teaching us that truth through our pain, we actually build a road for His salvation to come to us. This verse has ministered to me more times than I can count. It allows me to count the awful circumstance I am experiencing as joy (see James 1:2) because I realize that my God is teaching me something else about the perfection of His character. He is maturing me so that I can see Him where I did not before. The sacrifice of praise deepens my trust in the One whose love is perfect as I relinquish my will to His. God delights in showing Himself to be faithful and trustworthy when I praise Him sacrificially.

I have asked the Lord to make the pages of His Word spring to life when I read them. I used to think that these ancient stories which happened thousands of years ago were just stories. I thought that the biblical stories of women who lived in a culture like Leah and her sister had no power to speak truth and healing into my twenty-first century life. Yet, as I have submerged myself into the lives of Sarah, Hagar, Rebekah, Leah, and Rachel, I am astounded at how many parallels I see between their lives and my own. By the power of the Holy Spirit, I am able to see these women in a completely different light as He convicts me of choices that I have made in my own life that mirror theirs.

One thing I am convinced of: Every woman craves security. Maybe, like Sarah, we are willing to compromise the sacred like sharing a man with someone else in order to feel worthy. Like Hagar, maybe we panic easily as we find ourselves in yet another desert season when all that we have looked to for security has been taken from us. Or perhaps we keep secrets from those whom we should be the closest to and struggle with the need to manipulate to help us feel as though we are somehow in control as Rebekah did. We have only just begun to see the ugliness of jealousy's face between Leah and Rachel to obtain the security of one man's love.

You and I were never meant to do this life on our own. Instead of standing in awe that the Creator of the universe would desire a relationship with me, I have treated the Lord as though He were a heavenly Benefactor who needed to fulfill my desires before He could have my whole heart. There have been times during great crises that I have known that God is very real. I have even known how undeserving I am of His mercy. But that did not change my hard heart to completely embrace Him as my God.

When was the last time hope was the truest and deepest emotion that drove our thoughts and actions?

Which of the five women discussed above (Sarah, Hagar, Rebekah, Leah, or Rachel) do you most relate to in the season of life you are now experiencing? Have you come to realize that you have not relinquished complete control to the Lord in this area? Use this space to tell Him what is on your heart:

Find rest, O my soul, in God alone; my hope comes from him. He alone is my rock and my salvation; he is my fortress, I will not be shaken. My salvation and my honor depend on God; he is my mighty rock, my refuge.

Psalm 62:5-7

When was the last time our souls were at rest? When was the last time hope was the truest and deepest emotion that drove our thoughts and actions? When did we know, beyond a shadow of a doubt, that no matter what happened to us, we would not be shaken? It is only possible to have true rest, hope, and victory when we are convinced our salvation and honor depend on God, our mighty Rock and our Salvation. Something had happened at Judah's birth in Leah's heart. Had Leah truly learned that the love and security she craved would never be found in Jacob or in her children or was this awareness only momentary? We will learn the answer to that very important question in tomorrow's lesson.

Day Five – The House That Envy Built

A house is built by wisdom
and becomes strong through good sense.
Through knowledge its rooms are filled
with all sorts of precious riches and valuables.
Proverbs 24:3-4 (NLT)

As we start this lesson, I want us to ponder the following questions: How would you evaluate your own home? Are wisdom and good sense the strength of its foundation? Are we pursuing spiritual knowledge? What furnishes our home, precious riches and valuables that come from having the Lord as the Master of our homes or strife and jealousy?

I have been a mother for fourteen years. My husband has wisely observed since we became parents that our children were given to us by God to teach us two about ourselves. I have not always appreciated those lessons as they peel off motives that I would like to hide from the light of truth. Nobody exposes me and my weaknesses better than my children. I can espouse the virtues of patience, kindness, and gentleness and have my children rip off my self-righteous mask in less than one minute on any given morning as I bark at them through our early morning routine before they leave for school.

We bring our past experiences, our hurts, our expectations (right or wrong) to every relationship we encounter.

After nearly two years of motherhood, I was under the false impression that I had somehow mastered the ability of having this parent thing figured out: my wonderful first-born was obedient, polite and kind to others. That fantasy was shattered before his second birthday when my second child became old enough to defend herself from having a toy taken away from her. I noticed that her older brother became insistent on having the same toy as she did, even though he had been happily playing with something else and was surrounded with endless possibilities to keep himself occupied. Although my son could not explain what was going on in his heart over wanting what his sister had, I could easily empathize with his jealous behavior toward his sister.

People never react out of a vacuum. We bring our past experiences, our hurts, our expectations (right or wrong) to every relationship we encounter. I have asked the Lord to remove the scales from our eyes as we look at these often-too-familiar characters in the life stories of Abraham, Isaac, and Jacob. Without understanding why we continue to react in ungodly ways toward family members or friends, we are destined to keep repeating those same behaviors. The abundant life that Jesus promises is available to you and me (John 10:10) as His followers will continue to elude us. Life will continue to be joyless. Our relationships will continue to be marked by anger, bitterness, and strife.

We need to examine the foundation on which our relationships are built. Without understanding where we have come from, we will not understand where we are going and why. Our childhoods forever shape us as young women and beyond. We are going to ask the Lord to uncover what sort of home the wives of Jacob had built and, perhaps, discover something about our own homes in the process.

Before we begin, I wanted to share Psalm 19:7 with you as a prayer. I love the HSCB version of this verse:

The instruction of the LORD is perfect; reviving the soul; the testimony of the LORD is trustworthy, making the inexperienced wise.

I need some soul reviving and some wisdom in my inexperience and ignorance especially in matters of the heart and in my relationships! How about you? Holy Spirit, we are asking You for revival of our souls and wisdom in this lesson.

Circle any of the following words that have characterized your relationship with a sibling at one time or another:

jealousy competition hatred bitterness

unforgiveness hurt despair emotional distance

misunderstanding bickering apathy

Briefly describe the circumstances surrounding these emotions. You will not be asked to share this in your group:

Please read Genesis 30:1-24 and then answer the following questions:

What caused Rachel to be jealous of Leah in verse one and whom did she expect to be able to do something about her longing? What words did she use to describe the depth of her desperation if her longing remained unfulfilled (v. 1)?

What did Rachel do to get what she wanted in verse 3 that might lead one to believe she did not have ears to hear Jacob's rebuke in verse 2?

My sweet sister, maybe you and I have never considered building our families by encouraging another woman to sleep with our husbands, but I can certainly think of some humiliating decisions I have made in order to keep or get what I thought I needed. We have sacrificed the sacred for the urgent need we have. Some examples might be:

- Betraying a friendship
- Compromising our integrity in a dating or marriage relationship
- Pretending we are someone we are not
- Taking credit for someone else's work at our job
- Gossiping or lying to others to make ourselves look good

How many children came from Jacob's union with Bilhah, Rachel's maidservant, and what did each of their names mean (vv. 4-8)?

What insight do the meaning of the names give you about the way Rachel viewed her sister?

Scripture is not clear what Rachel felt vindicated about, but Naphtali's name leaves no doubt that Rachel viewed her sister as a threat and an enemy. She saw these children as a way to stay in the position of power over Leah. What happens when two wounded people believe they are justified in wounding the other? Let's read on.

How did Leah react to Rachel's fertility plan (vv 9-10)? Circle one:

Cried out to God

Treated Rachel with compassion

Decided to make it her own

Jealousy sees its victim through merciless and blind eyes.

What did she name her sons through Zilpah and what were their meanings and do you believe her sons' names were representations of her true emotional state?

There is hardly a biblical story that makes a better case than this one as to why jealousy is so destructive in our relationships. Jealousy sees its victim through merciless and blind eyes. Both women had reasons to choose to be content before choosing to become each other's competition. Rachel was beautiful and had the devotion of her husband which Leah longed for above anything else in her life. Leah was blessed with four strong sons while her sister lived with a barren womb that screamed to her daily about her worthlessness.

What does each of the following Scriptures reveal about the reason for the relational chaos between the sisters? Identify which sister fits with each passage:

Proverbs 30:15-16

Proverbs 30:22-23

If you and I are not immersing ourselves in the infallible Word of God, we are doomed to a life void of the knowledge of God's character and His power. We will repeat sinful behaviors. Scripture tells on people. Scripture exposes motives. Scripture gives us sound counsel on how to deal with others instead of making their sinful reactions our own.

Just when it seemed the situation could not get any worse, it did. What exchange took place between Rachel and Leah in Genesis 30:14-17?

Have you ever felt like you "sold" yourself to get something/one you wanted desperately? Use three words to describe how that made you feel:

What had happened to Leah as a result and what did she believe she was being rewarded for in verse 18?

Can I just shout, "What are you thinking, Leah?!" Where in the world did she ever get the idea that giving Zilpah to Jacob to sleep with was something to be rewarded for?

Remember the four situations in which the earth cannot hold up according to Proverbs 30:23? Write out the last situation given here:____.

As if the strain between the two sisters wasn't great enough, they had to complicate matters even more. Bilhah and Zilpah were no longer servants. They were now Jacob's third and fourth wives whose offspring were given full rights as sons of Jacob!

Scripture gives us sound counsel on how to deal with others instead of making their sinful reactions our own.

Record the meaning of Leah's sixth child's name. What did she still desperately hope that her sixth son might give her in the eyes of her neglectful husband (Gen. 30:19-20)?

My dear sisters, aren't we so like Leah? We want so much to believe that something we do or possess will bring us what we crave from another human being – unconditional love and someone who will convince us that we are significant. My heart and eyes well up in empathy for Leah and her plight because I have been Leah!

What does Psalm 62:7-8 have to say about this longing we all have?

This is not a question to respond to, but to ponder: when was the last time we stopped to pour out our hearts to Jesus instead of a human being who does not have the ability to love us as we want to be loved? We must understand that Jesus is the only One who can fill the aching void in our hearts that we look to fill with earthly relationships or possessions.

What was the gender and name of Leah's seventh child (Genesis 30:21). Tuck this fact away in your mind as you will learn more of this child soon in a future lesson:

What great event in Rachel's life happened in vv. 22 and how did she see the effect of this event on her personally in vs. 23? What did she ask God for in vs. 24?

My heart is welling up over the lavish mercy of our God. I had never seen this before, but I pray that what I am about to share will bless you. I have just passed through the most difficult season of my life. I had never seen how intimate and attentive God was to both of these sisters, even after they had both made such a mess of their lives and families. Someone in addition to me needs hope that Jesus is the Redeemer of shattered lives.

Fill in the action God took with each sister:

Leah: (vs. 17) God ______________________.

Rachel: (vs. 22) God ______________________.

With Leah, the Hebrew meaning of listen means "to hear, to listen, to obey, to heed with interest or attention." It also applies to hearing as a judge would hear a court case. My sister, do you need to know that your God is listening to your tears with tender and profound interest and attention? He is the ultimate Judge. When He says your trial is over, the trial will cease! But you and I have to hold on with eyes of faith during those days when we doubt He is even present in our circumstances.

Maybe you, like Rachel did for so many years, have lived with a flaw that has caused you great pain and disgrace. Maybe you made destructive choices for a season that you are still living with daily. Maybe you feel forgotten in other ways – you are single and want to be married or you also know the deep darkness of a barren womb yourself. Perhaps you or a loved one is struggling with a health issue. There are some days you don't know if God remembers you exist! Remember means "to recall, to call to mind." There is a glad day coming when you will know our Jesus did remember you and that He has recalled to mind your particular grief as you see first hand the work of His salvation inside the pain. Continue to burden Him with your unanswered longings. He is strong enough to carry them and will answer you at the perfect time.

Manipulation and competition should not play any part in our actions toward others if we are seeking to follow Jesus Christ. Today's peek into the competition between two sisters is the perfect example of how horrendous our relationships can be when we try to manipulate like Leah and Rachel did. Have you and I been guilty of the same impure motives in our relationships?

My darling sister, is there something we need to confess before the One who sees everything? We don't confess because God is ignorant of our deepest hearts. We confess to bring out into the light the toxic secrets that have caused or could cause destruction. I pray that you would know that your Redeemer, with whom you bare your soul is the same One who listens to and remembers you with boundless love. Let's dare to trust Him as we ask Him to make our divided homes into homes that display His power.

Fill in your name in the following blanks as we close today:

Remember these things, O ____________________, for you are my servant, O ____________________. I have made you, you are my servant; O ____________________, I will not forget you.
– Isaiah 44:21

Manipulation and competition should not play any part in our actions toward others if we are seeking to follow Jesus Christ.

WEEK THREE

A Hard Journey Home

Scripture does not record any miracle surrounding him, as was the case with Peter walking on the tempest toward Jesus. His relationship to Christ is not described like the apostle John's as the one whom Jesus loved. In fact, his name is mentioned only once in Scripture to indicate that he was one of the inner circle of the twelve disciples of Christ. Yet, what Jesus said about Nathanael would thrill my soul more than any other words He could say about me:

When Jesus saw Nathanael approaching, he said of him, "Here is a true Israelite, in whom there is nothing false."

John 1:47

Few decisions are more destructive than choosing to allow duplicity and lies to rule our actions. Presenting a false representation of ourselves to others in order to control or manipulate them for our own benefit has us playing a dangerous game.

It is very disconcerting when we discover and uncover deceit and false pretenses in those close to us. We will examine the dangers of running away from necessary confrontation in our relationships this week and witness the beginnings of life-long consequences stemming from deceit and favoritism in Jacob's family relationships.

We long for truth in our relationships. But more importantly, **God** wants truth to characterize our relationships. I pray that we will not only see others in this week's homework, but ourselves as well and ask God to help us to develop truth in the inmost places of our hearts. Like Nathanael, I want Jesus to be able to say about me:

"Here is a true follower of Mine in whom there is nothing false."

Day 1 – Deceit's Complicated Goodbye

I am praying that the Scriptures we have studied have been able to speak to us individually as we have studied the complexity of family dynamics in the lives of the patriarchs, Abraham, Isaac, and Jacob ... and in our own as well. I hope that we are ready to dive right in because we have much to cover today. This will be one of the longest portions of reading that we will do in a single day, but I believe we will glean insight from the long goodbye Jacob and his family had with his father-in-law, Laban.

Identify one or two areas in your own life that the Lord has spoken to you directly through the study of His Word so far. Record your thoughts in the margin.

Two building blocks of unforgiveness are betrayal and lack of trust on some level.

As we begin this lesson, what does Psalm 119:102 declare? Circle one:

God Himself teaches me.
My sin blinds me to truth.
God hears my cries.

My sweet sister, will you take a minute to invite the most competent, patient, and loving Teacher into this lesson with us? It inspires awe in me to know that God will do the teaching if I ask Him. When He teaches, the lessons remain. That's what we want!

To begin, we have to remind ourselves of the contract that existed between Laban and Jacob that was agreed to a month after Jacob first arrived in Paddan Aram. Why did the contract exist according to Genesis 29:16-20?

Jacob, the deceiver of his father and brother, had met his match in his father-in-law, Laban. After a wedding night "mix-up," Jacob found himself working twice as long for his father-in-law as he had originally agreed for one more wife than he wanted. We are continuing to look for well-established patterns of behavior that will help us understand why families function as they do. Two building blocks of unforgiveness are betrayal and lack of trust on some level. Betrayal often comes through deceit.

Deceit is defined in Webster's Dictionary like as: **"the act or practice of deceiving; an attempt or device to deceive; the quality of being deceitful."** Synonyms for ***deceit*** are listed as: ***cheating, cunning, fakery, fraud, and guile.***[1]

What do the following Scriptures say about deceit:

Job 27:4:

Psalm 5:6:

Psalm 32:2:

Psalm 101:7:

1 Peter 2:1:

We are going to observe several scenes of deceit and name those who are involved in each one as we read through Scripture today. There is no such thing as a "white" lie. A half-truth equals a whole lie.

Jacob had worked for fourteen long years for his two wives. In all that time, Scripture is silent about Jacob ever communicating with his parents back in Canaan. God had made a covenant with Jacob about being with him in Paddan Aram, but He the blessing that Jacob had deceitfully taken from his older brother, Esau, would be fulfilled back in the land of his birth. It was time to go home.

There is no such thing as a "white" lie. A half-truth equals a whole lie.

Please read Genesis 30:25-43. We will study this carefully together by answering the following questions:

What event caused Jacob to ask for Laban to send Jacob and his family on their way back to Canaan (vv. 25-26)?

What flowery enticements did Laban use to deny Jacob his request (vv. 27-28)?

Master manipulators do not come right out and say no. But you can be assured that the person who remains highest in the manipulator's mind is him/herself! Promises of reward or false flattery for cooperating are offered as bait. Jacob, however, was not new at this game! Realizing that after fourteen years, he had nothing to show for his hard work in the way of material possessions, Jacob devised a scheme of his own to remedy the reality that he would be returning to Canaan empty-handed.

What did Jacob request of Laban as payment (vv. 31-33)? Circle one:

Gold and silver   Forty servants   Laban's dark, speckled, and spotted livestock

Listen to what commentator Matthew Henry pointed out as a possible reason for Jacob's request:

"Some think [Jacob] chose this colour because in Canaan it was generally most desired and delighted in; the shepherds in Canaan are called Nekohim (Amos 1:1), the word here used for speckled..." [2]

What did Laban immediately do after he had agreed with Jacob's terms (vv. 35-36)?

If Jacob's blood pressure skyrocketed in anger after he learned about Laban's deviousness, we can surely understand. Laban had deliberately lied and made Jacob's desire of having his own flock nearly impossible to realize.

Instead of confronting Laban, what strange experiment did Jacob conduct (vv. 37-42) and what happened as a result (vs. 43)?

Let's continue reading Genesis 31 in its entirety.

What had Laban's sons' jealousy toward their brother-in-law's success caused (vs. 2)? Can you personally relate to feelings of envy from a family member?

Master manipulators do not come right out and say no.

After reading Gen. 31:3, share a time when God suddenly took you out of your environment (job change, move, graduation, etc.):

The problem was, Jacob was not the bachelor he had been when he arrived. Who did he include in the decision to move and what was their response (vv. 4-16)?

According to the response of Rachel and Leah, it appears no love was lost between daddy and daughters. I have a friend whose father has not considered her feelings as he has selfishly lived for himself after his divorce from her mother and consequent multiple marriages since then. The emotional distance between them is as wide as the Grand Canyon.

What did Jacob do in vv. 17-18?

The web of deceit soon became wider. A new deceiver was introduced - who was it and what did this person do?

The NIV says that "Jacob deceived Laban the Aramean by not telling him he was running away (vs. 20)." The pattern of running away from confrontation was nothing new to Jacob. Fleeing seemed the easiest way to leave the mess behind ... or so it seemed.

When was the last time you fled from a messy relationship? What was the result?

What did Laban accuse Jacob of doing after he had caught up with him in Gilead (vv. 26-28)?

Whom did Laban reveal restrained him from his power to harm Jacob and what did he want returned (vv. 29-30)?

What did Jacob rashly declare without knowledge of the truth in verse 32?

It seems Rachel had learned from her daddy how to deceive with a straight face. How clever to lie to Laban about having a female issue to hide the stole household gods she wanted to take to her new home in Canaan. He didn't look closely enough.

Write out the words that Laban said to Jacob in verse 49:

How would you describe Laban's emotions behind those words:

Affectionate
Calling for God's judgment
Heartbroken

Would you say that Jacob and Laban had reconciled by verse 55? Give reasons.

I was involved in a serious dating relationship in college. There was a necklace called "the Mizpah" necklace which was quite popular in the late 1980s. The one my boyfriend and I exchanged had the words printed on a gold circle that was split in half. He wore one half of the circle on a chain around his neck while I took the other half. The idea was that only when the two people wearing one half of the necklace would receive the blessing of God watching over each of them until they were together again.

The jewelry designer had taken Genesis 31:49 entirely out of context.

The Mizpah was not an affectionate blessing from Laban on Jacob! Laban was calling down a curse on Jacob's head should he abuse his daughters in any way. The relationship between the two men had deteriorated to such an extent that Laban did not trust Jacob anymore. Jacob felt entirely the same way about his father-in-law. Instead of the word *Mizpah* signifying a loving, whole relationship while the two men were apart from each other, the Hebrew word actually means *watchtower*. Why would anyone want a watchtower between them? In ancient and medieval times, a walled city would have a watchtower to be able to see an enemy from a long distance away. Jacob and Laban were no longer family in each other's minds; they were enemies.

What happens when deceit rules in our relationships? When we do not do what we promise to others? When we cheat and steal from each other emotionally? Trust is broken, perhaps forever, and unforgiveness takes root. Laban and Jacob would never see each other again. Leah and Rachel and all of their children lost a father and a grandfather that day when the watchtower was erected between the three generations. The family was fractured and broken. And only God Himself would know from then on what was happening in the families of Laban and Jacob because no communication is ever recorded in Scripture again between the two men or Laban and his daughters.

Why does God hate lying? Proverbs 26:28 says: *A lying tongue hates those it hurts, and a flattering mouth works ruin.*

Next time you and I feel justified in lying to, cheating, betraying or defrauding a family member or close friend, we need to remember the horrible cost those actions demand on our relationships. God never intended for families to be separated by watchtowers and walls. Speaking the truth in love is the first sledgehammer we can use against those walls. Let's stop hating each other with lies and false flattery in our families and honestly evaluate our own hearts' motives. What is the Holy Spirit telling us **we** need to do for healing to begin in our families? I pray for all of us to have the courage to obey.

Next time you and I feel justified in lying to, cheating, betraying or defrauding a family member or close friend, we need to remember the horrible cost those actions demand on our relationships.

Day 2 – Desperation's Great Gift

Desperation is a gift.

Did you just go back and read that sentence again? I surely would have shook my head in disagreement at that seemingly preposterous statement before God started teaching me what desperation can do for my relationship to Him. None of us want to appear to be desperate in front of another human being. Humans abuse us in our desperation.

King David knew the human heart all too well:

"I'm in a desperate situation!" David replied to Gad. "But let me fall into the hands of the Lord, for his mercy is very great. Do not let me fall into human hands." ***1 Chronicles 21:13 (NLT)***

What desperate situation (current or past) required you to beg for the Lord's mercy?

As Jacob watched Laban's caravan meander ever farther away from the family's campsite at Gilead, he may have breathed a sigh of relief that his father-in-law had left and his family was still intact. God had told Jacob to leave Laban and go back to Canaan (Genesis 31:3). God had not, however, been a part of anything that was deceitful between Jacob and Laban. That was all Jacob and Laban's doing. God does not tempt us to sin (James 1:13). God does not make our messes, but neither does He leave us in the middle of them. He is the Redeemer.

Why do you think Genesis 32:1-2 happened soon after the events of Genesis 31?

There have been times in my life where God has moved in with His undeniable presence, just when I least expected that to happen. Right in the middle of the muck and mire of the mess I had created. After assuring Jacob of His continued presence with him, God was ready to give Jacob the gift of desperation.

Please read Genesis 32:3-32.

What unresolved business lay ahead of Jacob before he could return home and how did he handle it (vv. 3-5)?

What did Jacob find out in verse 6 and what plan did he come up with (vv. 7-8)?

What did Jacob plead and to whom in verses 9-12?

Desperate is quite fitting to describe Jacob's emotional state. Let's remind ourselves of why Jacob was so fearful of this reunion by reading Genesis 27:41.

What was Esau planning to do twenty years earlier when Jacob had deceived Isaac for the blessing? Circle one:

Get revenge on his mother. Marry two more wives.
Kill Jacob.

What do the following Scriptures tell us about the character of God toward us?

Numbers 23:19:

Isaiah 44:21:

Hebrews 6:10:

We remind God of His promises to us in our prayers not for His sake, but for ours.

Jacob was terrified of what Esau's reaction was going to be to him at their first meeting. List what Jacob did in Genesis 32:13-21 in preparation for seeing Esau:

Would you call Jacob's gift to Esau slightly extravagant? What does Proverbs 18:19 reveal?

Have you known this verse to be true from life experience? Share here.

Broken trust, especially between family members or other close relationships, can sometimes lead us to act in ways that we would not normally act. When regret is our motive, we can go overboard trying to make things right, especially when we do not know how the other person is going to react to us. Fear driven by regret is rarely subtle. Some of my most humiliating reactions have been made this way.

What did Jacob do with his family and possessions in vv. 22-23?

I was blessed with two children in a span of thirteen months. When my second child was about six months old, I began to experience insomnia three or four nights a week. I had just begun seeking God earnestly by establishing time daily in His Word and praying more than just at mealtimes. I would lay there in the dark so incredibly frustrated at the fact that my mind could not or would not shut off. My children needed me to be well-rested and ready to meet their many needs the next day. My husband would fall asleep as fast as his head hit the pillow. I would listen to his deep breathing and watch as the hours would tick away minute by minute until the morning light. Sometimes I would doze for an hour or two until I heard one of my children crying impatiently to be changed and fed.

Desperate? You bet I was. Hot tears of anger would slide down my cheeks as the weeks of restlessness and lack of sleep turned into a month. I was secretly tempted to pinch my husband to wake him so that he could share in my misery in the dark. I never did because I knew Rob had an exhausting eleven hour day at work with the commute each way to downtown Chicago and we did need our bills to get paid!

During the fifth week of my insomnia, I decided my anger was doing no good to calm my racing mind. I started to pray. I would reflect on what God was teaching me in the monotony of motherhood tasks of dishes, laundry, and cleaning. I even started to praise Him for that concentrated time of aloneness when I could pour my heart out to Him. Something started happening ... slowly. My irrational fears over my children's safety started to dissipate. But the biggest change was that I could now see some of the lies I had believed about how God saw me.

Where did Jacob find himself and what time of day was it in verse 24?

Write out the second part of verse 24.

I have always read this verse in this way: *"Jacob wrestled with a man until daybreak."* No, the man wrestled with Jacob. Do you see the difference? Many biblical scholars believe that this man was no ordinary man, but the pre-incarnate Christ.

What did the man do to Jacob in verse 25 and why?

What did Jacob tell the man in verse 26?

What happens when God comes to wrestle with us? We cannot be left the same. Jacob's hip would never be the same. He would always walk with a limp from that day forward. Even though Jacob's hip was permanently affected, he continued to hold on to the man for the blessing he dared to ask for. Too often we do not endure the wrestling for the blessing. We give up far too easily as thoughts of abandonment, bitterness, and despair fill our minds and determine our futures.

My favorite version of Genesis 32:27-28 is out of the Amplified Bible:

27 [The Man] asked him, What is your name? And [in shock of realization, whispering] he said, Jacob [supplanter, schemer, trickster, swindler]!
28 And He said, Your name shall be called no more Jacob [supplanter], but Israel [contender with God]; for you have contended and have power with God and with men and have prevailed.

Have you and I ever wrestled with God? Or have we continually picked the safe and predictable path our whole lives – knowing of God, but never having really wrestled something out with Him until we saw the blessing? The "safe" path is anything but safe. It is full of the tragedy of never really understanding that Jesus Christ is more than a Savior to you and me. We think we want the road to stretch out smoothly in front of us for as far as we can see. No bumps, no deep, dark valleys. Just level and straight road. That kind of road tempts me to be lulled to sleep at the wheel as I am driving on a long trip. Spiritual apathy is a pit we can fall into when we live a life that is predictable without taking God up on the adventure to wrestle with Him over life's unanswered questions.

Spiritual apathy is a pit we can fall into when we live a life that is predictable without taking God up on the adventure to wrestle with Him over life's unanswered questions.

God knew what Jacob thought was his name – the one he answered to when called by the world: *schemer, trickster* and *swindler*. The cruel truth is that Jacob had come to believe that those names were his identity.

When you are alone with your accusing thoughts, what names have you thought were your identity? Some of mine have been: *insignificant, fat/ugly, bad mother, unintelligent, inferior*. Share here:

If we continue to wrestle with God and hold on for the blessing, that trial that we are walking through will bring us healing on the other side. But we can't let go too soon nor can we find healing on the path of little or no resistance!

For those of us who have accepted God's gift of salvation through the blood of Jesus Christ, what is the reward of being an overcomer according to Revelation 2:17?

A new name! A new identity! That is why God comes to wrestle with you and me – so that we can see ourselves as He does – not as the hopeless failures we may believe we are, but as one who contends with God and overcomes the stinging destruction of the consequences of our sin or the sins of others toward us.

If you and I are holding onto the poison of unforgiveness, we will never fully walk in the freedom of our new identity that cost Christ His life to give to us. Have you and I been given the gift of desperation in our circumstances? We can be so afraid of getting on the wrestling mat with Him. He doesn't come to wrestle with us to damage us. He has come to wrestle with us to give us a new identity as overcomers! Hallelujah!

If you and I are holding onto the poison of unforgiveness, we will never fully walk in the freedom of our new identity that cost Christ His life to give to us.

Day Three – The Ravages of Deceit

Is there really such a thing as a "white" lie? How about a half-truth? Does exaggeration count as a lie or can it be justified as just good story-telling? Scripture has much to say about the dangers we and our relationships will find ourselves in when the dark shades of untruthfulness color our speech and motives.

I believe that we live in a culture that emphasizes the loving nature of God, but rarely trembles at what He detests. I was ignorant of many passages of Scripture because I was scared to death or too bored to read the books in which the consequences for not obeying His commands were found. We *must* read the full counsel of God, and not merely pick and choose the parts we like or that make us feel good.

After reading Proverbs 6:16-19, list the seven behaviors God detests:

1) ____________________ 2) ____________________

3) ____________________ 4) ____________________

5) ____________________ 6) ____________________

7) ____________________

After wrestling with the man on the other side of the Jabbok until dawn, Jacob now faced one of the most difficult moments of his life – a potentially deadly encounter with his sworn enemy and brother, Esau. Limping because of his wrenched hip, Jacob was hardly in a position of strength should his brother take his pent-up rage of twenty years out on Jacob and his family.

Let's read Genesis 33:1-20. Pay close attention to acts of favoritism and/or deceit.

Using stick figures, draw and label Jacob's placement of his wives and children as they approached Esau (you only need to draw the women to represent families):

Do you believe their position went unnoticed by the four women and their children?

_____ yes _____ no. Who was the most highly favored?
Circle one:

Zilpah and sons Leah and family Bilhah and sons
Rachel and Joseph

How did Esau receive Jacob (verse 4)? How would you explain this? What exchange happened between the brothers in vv. 8-11?

What do you think Jacob meant by his words to Esau in verse 10?

Share a time when your fear of a situation was turned into joy because you knew the Lord had answered your prayers in an intimate way, leaving no doubt He had heard your prayers to Him about what had made you afraid:

Deceit never only takes what it set out to steal from another. Trust is also stolen.

How would you describe Jacob's response to Esau's invitation (verse 12) in vv. 13-15?

If you look at an ancient map of the land of Canaan during the time of Genesis, you will notice that Succoth was back over the Jabbok about ten miles north. Seir was about one hundred miles south of where Jacob and Esau had their reunion. There is no doubt from this text and Jacob's actions after seeing Esau that he had no desire to live within a close distance of his brother. Deceit and exaggeration misled Esau into thinking that Jacob would soon follow him to Seir.

What does Hebrews 12:15-17 give as insight into Esau's character that might have made Jacob wary of his family being closely entangled in Esau's life?

Maybe this hits close to home. Without naming names, is there a relative or close family friend that you would feel uncomfortable raising your children around? Please share why if you are comfortable doing so:

What stands firm forever according to Psalm 33:11?

Deceit never only takes what it set out to steal from another. Trust is also stolen. Jacob used deceit to get what he and his mother, Rebekah, wanted – the coveted birthright and blessing of the firstborn. Both panicked instead of trusting in the promise of the God who could not lie to Rebekah before the twins' birth regarding Jacob's position over his brother (see Genesis 25:23). God is all powerful and does not need us to manipulate a situation for our favor. He controls it all. Had Jacob waited for God to work out His plan, perhaps he could have been an honest man with his brother about his intentions instead of using his old pattern of deception to avoid confrontation.

God is all powerful and does not need us to manipulate a situation for our favor. He controls it all.

What life situation are you tempted to panic about and manipulate instead of waiting for the Lord to work out?

Which city did Jacob relocate his family to and how much did he pay for the privilege of pitching his tent there (Genesis 33:17-19)?

The altar Jacob built was called El Elohe Israel which means the *God of Israel* or *mighty is the God of Israel.* Slowly, Jacob was loosening his life-long grip on his old identity as a self-reliant schemer and embracing his new identity as an overcomer under the care of the God of his grandfather, Abraham, and his father, Isaac.

Day Four – Violence's Violation

I recently bought laundry detergent to refill a larger container that has a spout on the bottom. Unbeknownst to me, the side of the container had a small crack in the middle seam of the plastic. Because the previous level of the detergent had been below the crack, I thought that the integrity of the container was sound. Was I ever in for a big surprise! The detergent poured out of the invisible crack all over the top of my washing machine. I had to quickly come up with a solution to stop the mess that was quickly becoming larger and larger.

When favoritism is part of our family dynamic, there is bound to be a hemorrhage from the hidden cracks its destructiveness causes. Look back at the line-up you drew of the family as Jacob approached Esau (Genesis 33:1-2).

Fill in the rest of Genesis 34:1:
"Now Dinah, ____
________."

When favoritism is part of our family dynamic, there is bound to be a hemorrhage from the hidden cracks its destructiveness causes.

Remember, ladies, the children of the unloved wife, Leah? After realizing she had stopped being able to have children and giving her servant, Zilpah, to sleep with her neglectful husband, Leah had a baby girl of her own who completed her biological family. We are now going to read one of the most horrific chapters in all of the Bible where God's name is not mentioned one time and unspeakable acts are recorded.

Please read Genesis 34 in its entirety and answer the following questions:

What unspeakable act happened to Dinah? Circle one:

Killed by her brothers   Raped by Shechem   Banished from Jacob's family

My dear sisters, it is tempting to think that the world has grown more evil in the twenty-first century. The Bible is very clear that the unredeemed human heart has always been and will always be desperately wicked when left to itself (see Jeremiah 17:9). Horrific acts have been perpetrated against humans by humans since Adam and Eve's firstborn murdered his brother. What the world did not have before was immediate knowledge of the depth and breadth of the depravity of which men and women are capable. We have instant access through the media to stories that make our blood run cold in their inhumanity. One of the countless benefits of meditating on Scripture is that we are able to see that the ravages of sin have always been with us. Our sin-sick twenty-first century is nothing new.

Children learn what they live. Jacob's sons had been eye-witnesses to two major events in Jacob's life – the deceit involved in the fleeing of Jacob from Laban and the lie Jacob told their Uncle Esau about how he intended to follow Esau to Seir. The jealous rivalry between Rachel and Leah had produced eleven children by four different women. The biggest lessons in families are caught, not taught. Children learn by example more often than what they are told is the truth. Jacob's blatant favoritism and dysfunction as a parent had sown a bitter crop.

What did Jacob do when he heard about the violation of Dinah (verse 5)? How do you think this affected Dinah's brothers' reaction in verse 7?

Although Hamor and Shechem talked to both Jacob and Dinah's brothers, who made the proposal of circumcision to Hamor and Shechem? Why do you think this was so?

Looking at verses 13-16, why do we know that the brothers had no intention of carrying out their end of the bargain?

Children learn by example more often than what they are told is the truth.

Which named brothers carried out the murder of all the men in Shechem? Who was their mother? Who joined them in the looting of the town?

What startling truth is revealed about Dinah's location from the time of the rape to the time the murders were committed by her brothers (verse 26)?

What do the following passages say regarding hatred, jealousy and favoritism?

Proverbs 10:12

Proverbs 27:4

James 2:9

Mark where you have seen hatred (h), jealousy (j), and/or favoritism (f) in the following relationships in Jacob's family:

Jacob, Leah, and her children:

Jacob, Rachel, and her children:

Jacob and Laban:

Jacob and Esau:

Now I want us to do something very difficult. Write out the names of your parents, siblings, spouse, and children and repeat the exercise above marking where these destructive sins have appeared:

My sweet sister, are we going to have to be face to face with the carnage of a Shechem-like horror before we wake up to the devastation going on in our families? Where are we allowing our favoritism to show up in the lives of our parenting of our children? Do we secretly love one child over another? Is there hatred between us and a sibling(s)? Do we harbor toxic rage against a parent that has helped to build a rock-solid wall between us?

What was Jacob's response to Simeon and Levi's violent overkill to Dinah's rape in verse 31? Underline where the words *I, me, my, we* are used in this verse.

Then Jacob said to Simeon and Levi, "You have brought trouble on me by making me a stench to the Canaanites and Perizzites, the people living in this land. We are few in number, and if they join forces against me and attack me, I and my household will be destroyed."

Are you surprised at how many personal pronouns are in that one verse? Do you see any mention of Dinah and her father's grief over what had happened to her? Why would Jacob let his only daughter be kept hostage in the house of the man who had violated her? Self-absorption is a deadly addiction. The fear of what others think of us is a snare of enormous proportions (Proverbs 29:25).

If you are shocked and grieved at where the destructive sins of hatred, jealousy, and favoritism are uncovering their wretched faces in your own family, take heart my friend! Our Jesus is the Redeemer!

After reading Isaiah 58:6-12, let the Lord minister to you and show you what He wants you to do.

6 "Is not this the kind of fasting I have chosen:
to loose the chains of injustice
and untie the cords of the yoke,
to set the oppressed free
and break every yoke?
7 Is it not to share your food with the hungry
and to provide the poor wanderer with shelter —
when you see the naked, to clothe him,
and not to turn away from your own flesh and blood?
8 Then your light will break forth like the dawn,
and your healing will quickly appear;
then your righteousness will go before you,
and the glory of the LORD will be your rear guard.
9 Then you will call, and the LORD will answer;
you will cry for help, and he will say: Here am I.
"If you do away with the yoke of oppression,
with the pointing finger and malicious talk,
10 and if you spend yourselves in behalf of the hungry
and satisfy the needs of the oppressed,
then your light will rise in the darkness,
and your night will become like the noonday.
11 The LORD will guide you always;
he will satisfy your needs in a sun-scorched land
and will strengthen your frame.
You will be like a well-watered garden,
like a spring whose waters never fail.
12 Your people will rebuild the ancient ruins
and will raise up the age-old foundations;
you will be called Repairer of Broken Walls,
Restorer of Streets with Dwellings.
– Isaiah 58:6-12

Then you will call, and the LORD will answer; you will cry for help, and he will say: Here am I.
– Isaiah 58:9

It may seem so counterintuitive that obeying the commands in this passage of Scripture by helping others will bring about our own healing, but that is what the Word of God clearly says. How desperate are we for our families to be restored, for relationships that are broken down and lie in ruins to be built up again? Are you and I ready to step out of our comfort zone and surrender to whatever God may be asking us to do?

Are we ready for our Redeemer to redeem our own pain by comforting others with the gift of empathy?

As we close, I would like us to share with the Lord one or two verses from the above passage that His Spirit is speaking to our hearts most strongly about and why in the space below.

Blessings on you, my sweet sister!

Are we ready for our Redeemer to redeem our own pain by comforting others with the gift of empathy?

Day Five – A Fresh Start and Some Sad Endings

Vow: a solemn promise or assertion; specifically : one by which a person is bound to an act, service, or condition.[3]

On June 19, 1993, I made the most solemn vow to two persons that I have ever made. Before God and my husband, I solemnly promised that I would be faithful to my man until death parted us. Rob had pursued a relationship with me for over a year before I agreed to date him. Not one to ever play mind games, he had let me know the first time he asked me out that he was not interested in just dating, but marriage. I had just come out of a very serious relationship with a young man who I had felt I must say no to marrying. I was terrified of getting hurt again, so I refused Rob's requests for a relationship. I knew if I said yes to dating, I was saying yes to spending the rest of my life with him. It took me fourteen months to warm up to the idea. I am so glad that I finally came to my senses! The vow that joined me to him for the rest of our lives is the best one I have made outside of my decision to become a Christ-follower.

I am afraid that our culture laughs at the absolute seriousness of vows we make with our lips. There is a continual stream of stories of lawsuits in the paper because one party broke a contract and left the other high and dry. Divorce rates in the church are equal to those outside the family of God. One in two marriages will not live up to the vows made before God to stay together for a lifetime.

I am afraid that our culture laughs at the absolute seriousness of vows we make with our lips.

Match the verse with its reference:

It is a trap to dedicate something rashly and only later to consider one's vows.	Ecclesiastes 5:4
It is better to not make a vow than to make one and not fulfill it.	Ecclesiastes 5:5
When you make a vow to God, do not delay to fulfill it. He has no pleasure in fools; fulfill your vow.	Psalm 119:75
I know, LORD, that your laws are righteous, and that in faithfulness you have afflicted me.	Proverbs 20:25

Sometimes God allows us we to go through great personal suffering brought on by our own choices to not fulfill promises we have made to Him. God never lies. There is no darkness at all in His character. We cannot experience the abundant life that Jesus promised us by living a life of

disobedience. In His faithfulness, God will bring along circumstances which will force us to analyze where we are in our walk with Him when we are hurtling down a destructive path. Pain and hardship get our focus off of our own will and, hopefully, get us to take an honest evaluation of the slippery slope our sin has brought us to.

How has God, in His faithfulness, afflicted you to turn you from a destructive path or decision that you would not have turned from without experiencing pain?

Life has a way or getting blurred in our minds as the years pass. An experience that we have today might be the catalyst to remembering an event that happened long ago in our lives, but had become buried because of apathy, pain, or distance.

Please read Genesis 35:1-7. What did God command Jacob to do in Genesis 35:1?

Many biblical scholars, including Matthew Henry, believe that Jacob had bought the plot of land in Shechem after his reunion with Esau eight to ten years earlier.[4] What vow had Jacob made in Genesis 28:20-22?

That vow was now thirty years old. I wonder if you have had a traumatic experience that makes you avoid a once-familiar place. Perhaps you go out of your way to avoid the location because of the painful memories its nearness or visual remembrance brings. I periodically see lonely crosses that act as reminders to the horrific crash plunged into the grassy enbankment along a particular stretch of highway on which I am driving. I have often wondered if the victim's family is forced to travel that road often and be stabbed with a fresh reminder each time of what happened to their loved one(s). We can be assured that Shechem was no longer a place which Jacob felt comfortable calling home after the rape of Dinah and his sons' murderous looting of the city.

What did Jacob ask of his family members in Genesis 35:2-4 and does their response surprise you?

By the grace of God, what allowed the family to travel safely to Bethel to fulfill Jacob's vow according to verse five? Circle one:

An army of Arameans   The terror of God falling on others
Swift horses

Proverbs 16:7 tells us that, "When God takes pleasure in anyone's way, He makes even his enemies to be at peace with him." God did not take pleasure in any way over what happened to Dinah or what Simeon and Levi did when they took their rage out on the entire town of Shechem by killing all of its men. But when we start taking steps toward making a true heart change and seeking repentance over the destructive path we are on, God never withholds His grace and mercy. Godly sorrow that leads us to repentance (see 2 Corinthians 7: 10-11) is something that God takes great pleasure in. He is the God of second, fourth, even thousand chances. Jacob recognized that his family needed to be consecrated to the God of Abraham and Isaac, who was patiently waiting for him to make that decision.

What warning does Revelation 2:4-5 give us? How do these verses convict you of your spiritual state with the Lord right now?

Godly sorrow that leads us to repentance (see 2 Corinthians 7: 10-11) is something that God takes great pleasure in.

There are times when we need to take stock of how we are as a wife, a mother, a friend, and a neighbor. We can always come back to our first Love. He will never reject us even after the passage of several years or decades when we first made Him the promise that we would love Him foremost above anyone or anything else in our lives. In fact, He welcomes the prodigal wife, mother, friend or neighbor back to Himself as He runs to embrace us. How long has it been since we returned to our first Love or have we ever made Jesus Christ our first Love?

Who died in Genesis 35:8? ______________________________

The Bible can be full of what seems like random information at times. We have never heard the name of Rebekah's nurse before. Why would we hear about her now in her death? *Allon Bakuth* means *oak of weeping* in Hebrew.[5] Sometimes it is more important to pay attention to what Scripture doesn't say than what it does say. There was a person Jacob had left in Canaan thirty years earlier that he longed to see.

What were the last words he heard from this person's lips in Genesis 27:45 and who was this person? Underline the correct person and write out the verse underneath the name:

Ishmael, his uncle   Isaac, his father   Rebekah, his mother

Sadly, the reunion between mother and beloved son never happened. Scripture's silence about Rebekah leads us to believe that she had passed away some time before Jacob's return. As the family mourned Deborah under the oak tree, Jacob wept over having to bury the last tangible reminder of the mother he had been forced to leave thirty years earlier.

Write out the differences and similarities between Gen. 35:9-15 and Gen. 28:13-15, 18-19:

Similarities Differences

As painful as it must have been to lose Rebekah, the most painful goodbye that he had yet made in his lifetime was waiting for Jacob just around bend of the road toward Bethlehem. Why did Rachel die according to Gen. 35:18 and what did she name her second son?

My parents had a small single-engine airplane for many years that sat in a hanger on the top of the hill surrounding our mission station in Congo. Praise the Lord that none of our family members ever had to be flown by my father to the mission hospital of Vanga eighteen air minutes away. But the airplane was used many times for emergencies involving difficult Congolese births, most of which were successfully delivered. One unforgettable experience my parents witnessed was the death of a young Congolese woman who died on the airstrip trying to deliver a baby she had been in labor with for over three days. Her previous pregnancies had tragically ended with the babies dying in her womb, not able to be delivered because of the narrowness of her pelvis. The cries of anguish and grief of her family members still ring in my parents' ears to this day. The absolute agony and helplessness they felt over not being able to help her left an indelible mark on their souls.

Ben-Oni means *son of my sorrow*. *Benjamin* means *son of my right hand*. Do you think it was a wise idea of Jacob's to change the name Rachel gave her son and why?

How do you think our names can affect us?

Jacob set up two memorials on the long journey back to his father, Isaac. One memorial (verse 14) marked his joy over a now-fulfilled vow. The other marked his supreme sorrow over the grave of his beloved Rachel (vs. 20). I am sure that you and I can relate to setting up both sorts of memorials in our lives as well.

We have seen disproportionate anger in Simeon and Levi in their revenge against the Shechemites over Dinah's rape. What horrific act committed by the firstborn, Reuben, revealed more of the seeping hemmorrhage just below the surface of family relationships in verse 22?

Let's stand back a moment and analyze the status of Jacob's wives and children. Joseph and Benjamin were motherless. Reuben, the unloved wife's firstborn son, had become estranged from his father because of his incestuous relationship with his father's concubine, Bilhah. Matthew Henry writes of this tryst this way, "Though perhaps Bilhah was the greater criminal, and it is probable was abandoned by Jacob for it."

If Bilhah and Jacob were estranged, then what was the fallout for the two sons she had given birth to – Zebulun and Napthtali? It's enough to make your head spin, when you consider what dysfunction does to destroy our family relationships.

There are some points of irony that cannot be overlooked in Scripture. After coming home to his father, Isaac, and experiencing the death of his one remaining parent, who did Jacob reunite with at Isaac's funeral (verse 29)?

I wonder what kind of atmosphere prevailed between the brother's at their daddy's gravesite ten years after Jacob had promised Esau a visit to Seir? Don't you?

As we close today, no matter how peaceful or troubled our family relationships are or how hard our journey home to Christ has been, we have a tremendous promise in Scripture we can cling to:

But when he, the Spirit of truth, comes, he will guide you into all truth. He will not speak on his own; he will speak only what he hears, and he will tell you what is yet to come. He will bring glory to me by taking from what is mine and making it known to you.

John 16:13-14

But when he, the Spirit of truth, comes, he will guide you into all truth. He will not speak on his own; he will speak only what he hears, and he will tell you what is yet to come.

– John 16:13

What is it that the Holy Spirit has revealed to you about your own family relationships today and what is He urging you to do?

Nothing between my soul and the Savior,
So that His blessed face may be seen;
Nothing preventing the least of His favor,
Keep the way clear! Let nothing between.
– Charles A. Tindley, 1905 [6]

WEEK FOUR

Trail of Tears

O LORD, you have searched me
and you know me.
You know when I sit and when I rise;
you perceive my thoughts from afar.
You discern my going out and my lying down;
you are familiar with all my ways.
Before a word is on my tongue
you know it completely, O LORD.
Psalm 139:1-4

I have found such wisdom and comfort in the book of Psalms. It is not my first inclination to allow God to search my heart, but King David learned that intimacy and an understanding of God's constant presence in his life was the reward for his cooperation.

I have made a startling discovery in my walk with Jesus Christ – obedience to Him does not exclude me from heartache in this life. I know that if you and I sat across the table over a cup of coffee or tea, we would soon uncover the truth that both of us have had to walk our own trail of tears. Without the assurance that Jesus walks the trail of tears right beside us, we can be filled with a sense of confusion and hopelessness.

A home that is characterized by jealousy, deceit, and favoritism is like a volcano ready to erupt. Human beings do not react to a situation in an emotional vacuum. Each of us brings our past experiences, attitudes, and reactions into our interactions with others. If we do not give Christ authority over our past, we can make dreadful decisions in our present and future lives.

This week will begin with a look at the brokenness in the souls of Joseph's brothers which caused them to betray him on a level at which few of us will be able to relate. We will take a sobering look at the depths of depravity to which we are all capable of stooping if we do not allow the fear of God to restrain our sinful actions toward others. As follow Joseph's life as a slave in a foreign land, we will also wrestle with the question we have all asked of God when injustice is a part of our experience:

Why, Lord, why have You allowed this?

May you and I give the Lord complete freedom to search our hearts and pour His healing balm over the scars we have acquired as we have walked our own trail of tears.

Day 1 – Not My Brother's Keeper

What child does not long to be the favored one of all the siblings in a family? I will joke with my mother to this day that she loves me more than my sister and two brothers. We know that this silly statement of mine is not true, but I still say it to her every so often to get the grin out of her that appears on her face whenever I tease her in this way. I am a mama's girl through and through. Our voices sound so much alike now that I am an adult that many people, including my father, will think I am my mother when he hears my voice on the phone. We have the same mannerisms and gestures. The love of my parents has been a steadying force throughout my life. Somehow they were able to make us understand that they had no favorites among the four children. Now that I am a parent of three children, I understand what a difficult and delicate balance of love and favor they showed to each of us.

Write out the names of your parents/stepparent(s) and sibling(s) and/or half/step-sibling(s), and rate how close you are to each of them using the following number next to their names. Beside each name, briefly state the reason for rating each relationship as you did.

1) Estranged
2) Civil
3) Conditionally close
4) Good friend
5) Best friend

Underline every sin that has made its way into the family relationships of Jacob, his wives, and children that you have seen so far:

favoritism jealousy deceit murder rape incest
neglect suspicion hatred anger

Now, circle those sins above that you have seen to be sins in the preceding generations of Jacob's family, including those of Abraham and Isaac.

Please read Genesis 37:1-11.

Each of my children take impish delight in obeying me when I ask them to wake one of their siblings who is still in bed after he or she should be up. Nothing gives greater pleasure to one child than being able to tell on another one to me. There is something in the baseness of our sinful nature that takes secret pleasure in being able to give someone in authority a bad report about another.

Who gave the bad report about whom to Jacob in Genesis 37:2?

After reading verses 3-11, list the specific reasons why you believe the brothers "could not speak a kind word to [Joseph],":

By the time Joseph was born to Rachel, Leah's eldest sons (Reuben, Simeon, and Levi) were young adult men. Even if there was only one year spacing between the sons of Leah, Bilhah, and Zilpah, there would have been at least eleven years' separation between Reuben and Joseph after Dinah's birth to Leah. (Joseph's birth is recorded as happening after Leah gave birth to Dinah.) By the time we see Joseph as a seventeen-year-old in Genesis 37, his brothers, with the exception of Benjamin, most likely had families of their own.

What was the reason that Joseph's older brothers were not favored by their father?

What could they have done to change their standing in their father's eyes?

I can hardly think of a situation more heartbreaking than to be powerless to win the approval and affection of a parent whose rejection of a child is based on the disdain the parent has for the one who birthed the child. Joseph also had done nothing to deserve the blatant favoritism of his father except be born to the wife Jacob had loved most.

I can hardly think of a situation more heartbreaking than to be powerless to win the approval and affection of a parent whose rejection of a child is based on the disdain the parent has for the one who birthed the child.

What does Psalm 69:20 reveal as the consequence of a scorned heart?

What does the apostle Paul warn fathers not to do in Ephesians 6:4?

The New Living Translation (NLT) translates the word *exasperate* in the NIV as, "do not provoke your children to anger by the way you treat them." What Simeon and Levi did against the Shechemites was unconscionable and heinous, but usually disproportionate anger is a symptom of a far deeper problem – a bruised and battered heart. A perfect storm had been brewing for years whose furor was about to be unleashed in the form of a betrayal of staggering proportions.

Please read Genesis 37:12-18.

Where did Joseph think his brothers were and for what purpose?

What had they already started planning to do to Joseph in verse 18 when they saw him at a distance? Circle one:

Beat him up   Sell him to the slave traders   Kill him

I observed a tragic thread in reading through these verses. When Scripture described the relationship between the older brothers and Joseph, the words *hated him* were used three times (verses 4, 5, and 8). Hatred is a very powerful emotion.

Hatred is a very powerful emotion.

What does Proverbs 27:4 reveal to be the two other deadly emotions placed alongside anger?

Look back at the sins that you underlined and circled in Jacob's family on the first page of this day's homework. Were these three sins above ones you circled? Jealousy is so deadly in its power that no one can stand against its furor. After years of eating, sleeping, and breathing jealous thoughts, the brothers' minds were made up to get rid of Joseph once and for all.

After reading Genesis 37:19-36, what was the brothers' original plan in verse 20?

What brother successfully persuaded the others not to take Joseph's life? What was this brother's intention (verses 21-22)?

What three words would you use to describe the feelings Joseph may have experienced in the cistern?

Whose suggestion was it to sell Joseph as a slave to the Ishmaelites (vv. 26-27)?

It is interesting to note that twenty shekels of silver was a paltry sum to pay for someone who had never been a slave before. Joseph, stripped of the colorful coat his father had given him to show his delight in him as the favored son, was now led away as a person with no rights. And who had betrayed him? To Joseph's horror, the betrayal came from the brothers he had grown up with. No mercy was shown, although I am sure that Joseph's tears and cries for mercy rang in the brothers' deaf ears. I can not imagine how terrified and alone Joseph must have felt. We never imagine family members to betray us. No wound is so indelibly marked on our souls as that which is caused by those who should love us.

What brother was not there for the selling of Joseph and what did he do in response to what had happened to Joseph in verses 29-30?

After slaughtering a goat and mutilating the ornamented robe, the brothers fabricated a story to deceive their father into thinking that Joseph had been killed. The brothers had followed the sinful desires of their hearts and had dug themselves into a pit of lies so deep that they could not get out of the pit. I have tasted the bitter gall of trying to cover one lie with another lie in order not to come clean with the truth. Lies are like a ball and chain that we drag around. Unfortunately, we can become so accustomed to lying that we ourselves do not recognize the truth anymore.

We never imagine family members to betray us. No wound is so indelibly marked on our souls as that which is caused by those who should love us.

What was Jacob's reaction to seeing the coat the brothers brought to him? We will revisit this in more detail in the next weeks of the study.

Joseph was as good as dead to the family. The brothers, so blinded by their misplaced anger against Jacob and his blatant favoritism toward Joseph, had devised a scheme to send the source of their intense hatred away from their father forever. They had convinced themselves that by selling Joseph, they had rid themselves of the source of their pain in their relationship with their father for good. Deceit had become the foundation of how the family had dealt with conflict. We have seen its ugly face many times in this study already. Although Joseph may not have been physically present anymore, the brothers were going to tragically realize that they had not rid themselves of him, but that their viciousness toward Joseph and the cover-up would cause them to be haunted by their brother's memory every day of their lives.

What does Proverbs 14:12 reveal about the consequences of our actions?

You and I might believe we have every right to:
- gossip about a co-worker
- violate trust towards an apathetic husband/boyfriend
- refuse godly rebuke/counsel
- betray someone's confidence because he/she angered us
- nurse a grudge
- confront without speaking the truth in love

In every single scenario above, we can be sure we will experience death in those relationships. Instead of finding relief by taking part in the sins above, we will tragically find that we have only added pain to our lives.

Dear friends, never take revenge. Leave that to the righteous anger of God. For the Scriptures say, "I will take revenge; I will pay them back," says the Lord.

Romans 12:19 (NLT)

Who do you and I want to rid our lives of in our daydreams of revenge? We cannot let the enemy deceive us into thinking that revenge on our part would take care of the pain we have been feeling. If we step in and meddle with what the Lord is wanting to do in us and that other person, we may actually add to our suffering with regret over not letting God intervene for us. Our God is just. We must believe that even when we cannot see His justice in our circumstances. He has a plan that He is working out for our good. Any action on our part to "help" Him will only be interference and will, ultimately, be detrimental to us.

Day Two – A Sordid Start

I will guarantee for those of us who were raised in churches that used flannel-graph boards to help little minds visualize Biblical characters and events that today's story never made the acceptable list of children's Sunday School lessons. If we were to give a movie rating to the content of the thirty-eighth chapter of Genesis, we would not be able to rate the story we are about to delve into any lower than Restricted. I laugh when those who are ignorant of the Word of God declare that its story lines are predictable, boring, and irrelevant. Today's lesson speaks to the immutable character of God and His power to redeem the messes in which we become ensnared.

What traumatic event happened in yesterday's lesson that affected Jacob's family permanently? Complete the following sentence by circling the correct answer:

Joseph's brothers...

killed him and lied to Jacob

sold Joseph to the Ismaelites

plundered a city

Who had suggested to the others that this is what should be done in Genesis 37:26-27? ______________________________

I grew up in a culture in which women had very little in the way of personal rights.

Sometimes Scripture takes a break in the story line to elaborate on a major character's life or attitude. We are going to press pause on the story of Joseph to find out more about the brother whose idea it was to sell him as a slave. God, in His infinite wisdom, has the right to decide what and how much we should know about any one person or situation in Scripture. You may be confused at how today's lesson will fit into the overall story of forgiveness, but please trust that all Scripture is inspired by God and is useful for us (2 Timothy 3:16). Today's subject matter is worthy of our attention and study because He preserved it for us.

I grew up in a culture in which women had very little in the way of personal rights. In Congo, if a son was born into a family, he would be educated over a daughter. Women are called the tractors in Congo. We Americans would bristle under that title, but it is the reality in Congo. Women do most of the manual labor in Congolese culture. Their personal happiness or intelligence are rarely taken into consideration. A daughter's opinion means even less to the father and uncles who are making important life decisions for them such as marriage and educational opportunities. As female members of the western world, we take for granted having a voice in all decisions that pertain to our lives. Congolese women know no such freedoms.

We must approach today's lesson as though we were living in America in colonial days, before women had the right to vote or to inherit property. A woman and her children would be left destitute should her husband die before her sons were of adult age. We must see today's lesson through the eyes of the culture and time of our story.

Read Genesis 38 in its entirety and make observations in the margin of anything in the story that strikes you as unconventional/unusual or severe in a person's harshness towards another.

Compare Genesis 38:1 with Genesis 37:28. Name the brother mentioned in each verse and write "involuntarily" or "voluntarily" next to how he was separated from his brothers and each brother's destination each after the separation.

To do something voluntarily makes all the difference in the world, doesn't it? I may not like having to go somewhere, but I will despise the experience all the more if I am forced against my will to go there.

What nationality was the woman whom Judah married according to Genesis 38:2 that neither his grandfather, Isaac, nor his father, Jacob, had married?

Although this story predates the law being given to Moses, what was the warning the Lord gave the Israelites about intermarriage with other nations in Deuteronomy 7:1-4?

Share a relationship in which a Christ-follower married an unbeliever and how this affected the couple's unity and priority to growing in the believer's faith:

How many sons did Judah have? By whom did the two eldest die?

After reading Genesis 38:11-12, list the reasons why you might think Tamar knew Judah was not going to make good on his promise to her:

Deceit is so vile because it undermines trust. Look at what Scripture says about God's trustworthiness:

1 Samuel 15:29:

Psalm 55:18:

Malachi 3:6:

James 1:17:

You and I have a great temptation to believe that God is as fickle in His promises to us as human beings have been to us and we have been to others. Many women chafe under the idea of God being their heavenly Father because they had such a poor example of a loving earthly Father. Hear me, please! Your heavenly Father does not have the sinful tendencies of a human being. He does not lie. He does not revoke promises He has made to you. He does not hold confessed sin against you. He is not cunning or crafty or evil. There is no darkness to His glorious Person.

What did Jesus declare just before He died in John 17:17?

Deceit is so vile because it undermines trust.

In what area of your life are you having difficulty believing that God is trustworthy? Is your difficulty based on the character of others or of God?

Glancing back at Genesis 38:13-19, to what lengths did Tamar go to conceive?

Do you believe that promiscuity motivated Tamar's actions? If not, what did?

I do not believe that Tamar was promiscuous. She was not a hot-blooded woman who set out to have an intimate relationship with her father-in-law. She was desperate. If she had no children, her line would be completely severed. Jacob's son, Judah, had continued to deceive and avoid her right to be married to his third son, Shelah.

In my struggle to understand what God is doing as I wrestle with forgiving others, the Lord has revealed to me that *I do not know the whole story behind the pain inflicted on me.* I do not have the capability to judge motives. I do not know how the Lord is going to redeem not only the hurt in the other person's life for His glory, but in mine as well. I only see my one-sided perspective and am selfish enough to believe that I should get the revenge I want (in the way I want it!).

Did Tamar sin when she slept with Judah? Yes. Did she deceive also? Yes. Did God allow her to live while He killed her two previous husbands for their sin? Yes. Do I understand the way He works? NO! My responsibility is not to have the Lord figured out, but to trust Him with what I don't understand.

God has the right to be merciful to whom He wants to be merciful. And I cannot, for one minute, say that He has not allowed His mercy to triumph over the judgment I should have received for my actions. God alone judges the motives of the heart. He alone is able to make a righteous judgment - every time! Even when His judgment does not appear fair to me. I have to decide if I am going to let God be God or if I am going to try to sit on His throne and decide what I do not have the full knowledge about.

Write out Deuteronomy 32:4:

My responsibility is not to have the Lord figured out, but to trust Him with what I don't understand. God has the right to be merciful to whom He wants to be merciful.

It's so easy to say this truth when life is going our way. It will be a supreme test to believe this when difficult circumstances demand our trust in God's ability to always be faithful and upright. We must exercise faith to believe that He is incapable of doing anything wrong when we are wrestling with difficult matters of justice in our lives.

What injustice in your life, my friend, are you struggling to believe that God reigns over in His sovereignty?

What did Judah want to do to Tamar after he found out she was pregnant (Genesis 38:24)?

What did Judah say in verse 26 when Tamar produced evidence of the father of her child?

Which twin was the first one born in verses 28-29?

What good could come out of such a sordid tale of deception, incest, and immorality? None whatsoever if our unsearchable God did not have a plan to redeem even a mess as big as this one. This was not the end of Tamar's story.

Read Matthew 1:1-6 to find out how God remembered Tamar in Scripture.

Is Tamar remembered forever as a sinful woman who had an incestuous relationship with her father-in-law? No! Tamar was one of three foreign women (including Rahab the prostitute and Ruth the Moabitess) whom God chose to include in the most important family line this world has ever known – the line of Jesus Christ, the Son of David, the Son of God, who is the Redeemer of all sin. Praise the Lord that Jesus' human family tree was as dysfunctional as ours. How would we be able to relate to our faithful High Priest otherwise?

As we close, let's read Hebrews 2:16-18 and thank our Jesus for what He has done for us. He is fully able to redeem the sordid parts of our life stories as He did with Tamar's to include us in a plan that we could not even imagine if we will let Him be God in our lives. Our story isn't over yet, either. Hallelujah!

Our story isn't over yet, either. Hallelujah!

Day 3 – I Cannot Sin Against God

I am horrified at the temptations my children are faced with at their ages on a daily basis. My ten-year-old knows words and their meanings that I did not fully comprehend until my high school or college years. What was only talked about in whispers is now proclaimed unabashedly with no respect for what is sacred according to Scripture. My sister-in-law and I have committed to praying one day a week for our children as they face the mine fields laid down by a culture that continually tries to persuade them that there is no such thing as absolute truth. A culture that laughs at moral purity and tries to make them feel like social rejects if they are striving, with the Holy Spirit's help, to save the gift of their virginity for their future spouses. I thought the pressures were intense twenty-five years ago, but I never had to face what my middle-schoolers and elementary age child are exposed to through media, their teachers' beliefs, and the pressure of their peers.

What do you believe is the greatest pressure young people face today?

I am horrified at the temptations my children are faced with at their ages on a daily basis.

What does 1 Corinthians 10:13 promise us when we are tempted? Circle one:

A distraction   An escape   A once-for-all solution

We have looked at the moral depravity of Judah, the brother who came up with the idea to sell Joseph into a life of slavery. Today, in sharp contrast, we are going to find hope that someone committed to purity will be able to find the escape that Scripture promises to all of us when facing a great temptation.

I wanted to ask us all a question that we need to keep in the forefront of our minds during this lesson:

Why do we do the things we do? What drives us to obey the commands that God has set up for us? Our answer to these questions is going to deeply affect our perception of whether what God asks of us is to deprive us of fun or whether He is protecting us and providing peace through our obedience. The first perception will make His standards seem burdensome and may even make us feel as though we are being deprived. The second will give us fortitude to stand strong in the face of a temptation in which we may never be found out publicly.

How does 1 John 5:3-4 define our love toward God?

Check the ways obedience has sometimes felt burdensome to you:

____ Taking a stand for God in a public setting (school or the workplace)
____ Denying yourself the opportunity to watch a compromising movie or television show in a group of friends
____ Not attending an event/party because of possible temptations
____ Other: ____

Are you able to identify with the attitude of the psalmist in Psalm 119:32? Why or why not?

 Scripture holds up a mirror to our souls and shows us where we are deceiving ourselves. What does 1 John 2:3-4 reveal to us about the importance of obedience?

Ouch. I can think I am doing all the "right" things that a Christian is supposed to do – go to church, pray, read my Bible, even be involved in a Bible study. But the hard-to-swallow truth is that My obedience to God's commands or lack thereof is the barometer of my love for Him. I have to ask myself continually if the words *I love You, Lord,* coming from my lips are true when held up to this biblical definition.

My obedience to God's commands or lack thereof is the barometer of my love for Him.

Before we dig into our story today, let's refresh our memory with Joseph's bio. Fill in the following blanks:

Age (Genesis 37:2):
Relationship status with his father (Gen. 37:3):
Relationship status with his brothers (Gen. 37:4):
Reason for coming to Egypt (Gen. 37:28):

Joseph had gone from being the favored son of his father to a slave in Egypt. At home, he was shown overt favoritism from his father – the reason why his brothers could not even say a kind word to him. In an act of utter and unimaginable betrayal, he was sold, by his own brothers, to Egypt as a slave where he suddenly had no rights at all. Oh, and he was not even out of his teenage years.

We live in a society which gives us permission to blame everyone else but ourselves for our actions and decisions. The major talk shows would not have their daily sordid fodder if bitter individuals were not willing to come forward and expose all their dirty laundry in front of a television audience. These persons blame their upbringing, their lack of opportunities, or their school environment for the sins in which they are involved. We are quick to slap a psychological syndrome on someone to explain why that person acts in a vile manner. Girlfriends, we have refused to call sin by its true name. Look at the mess we are in!

Joseph had every reason to feel bitter. His young life had been marked by some of the deepest pain imaginable. Yet, the prayer of my heart is that we are going to see what preserved his integrity when faced with a temptation that to which many of us may have fallen prey had his circumstances been our own.

Let's read Genesis 39:1-5 and list what we discover about Joseph in these verses.

Who else took notice of Joseph and what did this person demand of Joseph in verse 6-7?

I had a wonderful friendship with a young man in college who was one of the most physically attractive people I have ever met. Despite his appearance, my friend remained humble and unfazed by the constant female attention he received due to his handsome face. There was not an arrogant bone in his body. Our friendship continued after we both had transferred to different colleges. He confided in me that outward attractiveness had proven to be a danger to him and had put him in a potentially compromising situation with a very wealthy woman twice his age who had posted a job in her home that he had taken. She had advertised the need to have someone help her clean. He soon realized she had very different intentions for him once he was in her home. She brazenly propositioned him on the spot.

Give the reasons that Joseph gave for his refusal in verses 8-9?

Dr. Andrew Schmutzer makes this stunning observation about these verses:

"Our integrity in sexual matters depends on the strength of our non-sexual relationships. The reason why we often cave on God's standards is because we don't have any horizontal commitments either."[1]

How persistent was Potiphar's wife in her seduction and what steps did Joseph take as a safeguard against the temptation (verse 10)?

Ladies, are we trustworthy when we know no one is watching us? We need to take a long, hard look at our integrity in those horizontal relationships God has given us. If secrecy and lack of accountability characterize our lives, Satan will gain a foothold. I was thinking about how this may play out in our lives:

1) Viewing illicit material through the media, literature, or internet because we think we can hide our addiction and rationalize that the images/situations are not real.

2) Compromising our integrity with a member of the opposite sex at our job because we foolishly believe that our sexual banter/flirtation is harmless. We foolishly deceive ourselves into thinking that our spouse (or his) never need know.

3) Slowly compromising our purity in a dating relationship because we are spending time alone together in a place where we know no one will help keep us accountable.

I guess an even bigger question we need to grapple with is *who* is trusting us to resist sexual temptation? Whose world would be devastated should you and I not diligently guard the preciousness of unbroken trust? I have three children who expect me to be faithful to their daddy, even when no one is looking. In a culture which tells me I have the right to fiercely guard my independence and live by my own rules, the seriousness by which God considers my marriage vows can quickly become buried in my own self-absorption and quest for pleasure.

Whose world would be devastated should you and I not diligently guard the preciousness of unbroken trust?

I made a covenant to Robert Michael Lantz on June 19, 1993 to "forsake all others and keep [myself] only unto him so long as we both shall live." My fear of God makes me tremble at the ramifications of giving in to the temptation to be disobedient to Him in this area. Sin is tantalizing only for a season and, in the end, its poison leads to death and destruction. There are shows I do not watch. I am selective in the music I listen to. Why? Because I am following a legalistic Christianity of do's and don't's? No, because I know the state of my own sinful heart. I know how my flesh will obsess over and long for what is forbidden. I can too easily commit emotional adultery.

After reading 1 Corinthians 10:8-12, what does verse 12 specifically warn us to understand about ourselves?

What safeguards have you intentionally put in place to guard yourself against sexual sin?

Joseph had Potiphar's trust horizontally. Joseph held that trust in honor far above the heady temptation to sleep with the wife of his master – remember, Joseph was only seventeen or eighteen years old! Potiphar had withheld nothing from Joseph except for his own wife. Do we cherish the trust we have with those who look to us to be women of integrity above the tempting snares of sexual sin and the pit of self-pleasure or gratification? If our eyes could only see what fire we are playing with when we compromise sexually, I believe we would understand what Joseph did: ***"How then could I do such a wicked thing and sin against God? (Genesis 39:9)"***

I wish that obedience was always followed by justice. It is one of the greatest heartbreaks known to Christ-followers that this sin-sick world does not applaud godly decisions.

After reading Genesis 39:11-20, what ultimately happened to Joseph for the honorable actions he took in this passage?

Makes you want to scream, doesn't it? Surely all of us have tasted the bitterness of betrayal and deceit on some level, although I have never gotten an unfair prison sentence as a result of someone's undeserved vindictiveness. Why would God allow such a travesty to happen in Joseph's life (and perhaps in ours as well)? There are some answers we will never have in this lifetime, my dear sister. But I do know this – that the promise Jesus gave to the apostle Peter is being given to us right now in this trembling moment that demands faith:

Jesus replied, "You do not realize now what I am doing, but later you will understand."
John 13:7

Can we hold on until that day, my sister? Can we trust those injustices to the One who is the righteous Judge and who will administer His justice perfectly one day? Joseph had no idea how this testing of his faith that demanded his painful obedience would ultimately allow God to reward his fidelity in such a breathtaking way years later. Neither do we know the heights, to which those seeming injustices that have happened to us will lead us. That is for a time in the future. Now is the time for us to show the Lord our God our love for Him by our obedience – whatever the cost.

Faith alone will provide the strength we need to continue to trust in God's promises and in the faithfulness of His character when betrayal and injustice comes knocking at our door. We must believe that what we see with our physical eyes is only temporal, but what we do not yet see is eternal (2 Corinthians 4:18). That belief will be what we cling to when unjust circumstances seem to mock our obedience to continue to trust our God when our world is falling apart around us.

This is love for God: to obey his commands. And his commands are not burdensome, for everyone born of God overcomes the world. This is the victory that has overcome the world, even our faith.
1 John 5:3-4

This is love for God: to obey his commands. And his commands are not burdensome, for everyone born of God overcomes the world. This is the victory that has overcome the world, even our faith.
1 John 5:3-4

Day 4 – The Necessity of Telling the Truth

We have seen the dreadful and unfair consequences of a vicious woman's lies in the life of Joseph. We live in a society that proclaims truth as being whatever truth means to each individual. Our culture rebels under the fact there is absolute truth in the Word of God. Unfortunately, we have seen first-hand how faulty that thinking is as the innocence of Joseph's name was slandered for a wrongdoing he did not commit. We are going to see in today's lesson if Joseph decided to tell the truth when the truth was not pleasant to reveal.

Let's remember the context of our story by reading Genesis 39:20-23.

I cannot imagine how dreadfully lonely Joseph must have been in a foreign culture in which he had now dropped in status from slave to prisoner. Let's stop for a moment to think about Joseph's situation. Youth is characterized by optimism, even when the optimism is unfounded. After weeks turned into months and months turned into years, Joseph's faint hope of rescue by his father would have slowly vanished. His brothers had led his father, Jacob, to believe that Joseph was dead.

Hiding information and being deceitful with one another are two things that dysfunctional families do best, after all.

What had the Lord commanded Joseph's grandfather, Isaac, not to do in Genesis 26:2-3?

Joseph's father, Jacob, would have been well aware of that promise given to his grandfather. After his long journey back to the land of Canaan after twenty years away living near his father-in-law, Laban, Jacob had no reason to leave his homeland again to travel to distant Egypt. Did Joseph wonder during those first years in Egypt if his brothers would come clean and tell their father the truth of what had happened to him? Or did Joseph know in his heart that he was as good as dead to his family from the beginning of his slavery knowing that his brothers would keep the horrible secret of their betrayal of the brother they hated to themselves. Hiding information and being deceitful with one another are two things that dysfunctional families do best, after all. Being confined to a prison must have given Joseph many hours to think about all that had transpired to bring him to a land in which his father would not think to look for him and to a prison for a crime he did not commit. Joseph could have easily slipped into the darkness of despair.

What does Genesis 39:21 specifically tell us happened to Joseph in prison?

The trust that Joseph had held in high esteem for Potiphar was now returned to him through the warden of the prison who trusted Joseph implicitly. God sometimes blesses us with favor in the most unlikely places.

What does Isaiah 45:2-3 reveal? What have been some of the treasures you have received during the darkest moments of your life (e.g. new perspective, sensing God's presence, realignment of priorities with God's, etc.)?

Let's continue by reading Genesis 40:1-4.

The prison in which Potiphar had placed Joseph was one in which royal prisoners were held. Verse 4 also gives us insight into the baker and cupbearer of Pharoah being attended and served by Joseph. While Joseph had few rights as a slave, this was not likely a prison of physical torture. Joseph continued to serve others, something which was greatly blessed by the Lord.

Let's remind ourselves of a detail we may have missed when we were first introduced to Potiphar. Compare Genesis 39:1 with Genesis 40:4. Who made the decision to give Joseph charge over the Pharoah's two new prisoners?

The writer of Proverbs 5 warned his sons to stay away from an adulterous woman. The entire chapter gives specific actions, behaviors, and attitudes of someone in the habit of seducing men. Certainly Potiphar's wife, with her incessant propositioning of Joseph, devious ways, and deceit, give me cause to believe that Joseph may not have been the first intended victim of her seduction. Potiphar's image and Joseph's low status as a slave demanded retribution of some sort towards Joseph. If Potiphar truly believed Joseph was guilty of the attempted rape of which Joseph had been accused, his decision to put Joseph in charge of the cupbearer and baker hardly seem to fit with a man bent on avenging his wife's honor. Joseph should have been put to death.

After reading vv. 5-8, what do you tend to do when you see someone depressed when you are also facing a difficult season of life? Circle all that apply:

Avoid him/her Offer comfort by listening Become annoyed with him/her

Underline the choice above that Joseph made toward the two men.

What was the specific reason that the two men were downcast and write out the words that Joseph gave in response to their sadness (verse 8).

For three generations before him, starting with his great-grandfather, Abraham, continuing with his grandfather, Isaac, and finally his father, Jacob, God had appeared to each one to assure them that He was with each man. Joseph never got such a visitation. Yet, he chose to continue to believe that God was all powerful and gave Him the glory for the interpretations of the dreams he was about to hear. It is amazing to consider that of the four generations of Joseph's family, Scripture is silent about flaws in Joseph's character. Instead, his suffering is highlighted. The mystery of God's plan for his life is a witness to the following verses:

Oh, the depth of the riches of the wisdom and knowledge of God! How unsearchable his judgments, and his paths beyond tracing out! "Who has known the mind of the Lord? Or who has been his counselor?"

Romans 11:33-34

After reading Genesis 40:9-19, please list the dream of each of Pharoah's officials and its meaning:

The Dream	The Dream's interpretation by Joseph

Which interpretation would you have struggled to deliver?

Joseph did not sugarcoat the baker's fate in any way. I would have found giving that interpretation to be almost impossible to relay to the baker.

Is there someone whom the Lord is urging you to have a difficult conversation with and you are dragging your feet because you are fearful of their reaction?

Most of my daydreams when I was a young girl, teenager, and single young adult centered around the day I would finally meet the man who would sweep me off my feet. I had even made a list of the physical feature and quality traits he would have (so Shawn, I know!) I imagined the first time I laid eyes on him to be romantic, for the bells and whistles to go off, and my heart to be utterly captivated by him from the moment I saw him. That was not the way it happened at all!

I moved to the same college town in which my sister was spending her senior year and decided to get connected to a Bible study with a local church. My decision to join the study may sound really spiritual. Let me assure you that the main reason I wanted to attend the Bible study was to, hopefully, meet some nice, eligible, Christian young men. I was, after all, the ripe old age of twenty-three. I was convinced I had already missed my best opportunity to be married because I had graduated from college as a single woman.

I had scanned the few young men in the circle and did not find anyone who immediately caught my eye. A young man named Rob Lantz asked me if he could walk me to my car, but I thought nothing more of his request than just a friendly gesture.

Rob had a totally different idea! For the next ten months, he persistently asked me out. I was not interested. His intensity scared me. He did not play games and was very honest about his feelings for me – qualities I did not appreciate at the time.

I finally agreed to attend a minor league baseball game with him the following summer. He sat with undivided attention as I related to him my growing up years in the Congo as a missionary kid. As he pulled up into the parking lot of my apartment building, he turned to me and, with gentleness, stunned me with the following words:

"Shawn, I think that some of the behaviors I have seen in you do not line up with someone who says she loves Christ."

What a romantic thing to say! I sat there completely stunned. To add insult to injury, he then asked me if I wanted to pray with him. For the first time, someone had seen through the games I had been playing as a Christian and had called me out on my behavior. I could not have been more furious.

What do the following verses tell us about the power of telling the truth, even when it is difficult? Match the reference with the correct verse:

Psalm 34:12-13	The truth will set us free.
Zechariah 8:16-17	A lying tongue lasts for a moment.
Proverbs 12:19	Keep your lips from speaking lies.
John 8:31-32	Speak the truth to each other.
Ephesians 4:15	Speak the truth in love.

God places people in our lives that believe the truth of His Word in the above verses. Psalm 141:5 says,

"Let a righteous man strike me — it is a kindness; let him rebuke me — it is oil for my head; let my head not refuse it." (ESV)

Sometimes we are angry for the wrong reason. Wounded pride is not a valid reason to withhold forgiveness. Are you struggling to forgive someone who had the courage to confront you over an ungodly behavior? Have you examined your hurt against the truth of Scripture? Is your anger justified according to the above Scriptures?

Listening to Rob's concern for me that evening in the parking lot, I knew that this man truly cared for my spiritual well-being that outweighed his desire for us to have a relationship. Although I was angry and hurt that he had confronted me, I tucked the rebuke away to be evaluated later that fall when I was deciding whether I could be married to him or not. Of all the young men I had dated, not one of them had ever respected Scripture as much as Rob did. He was in love with me; yet, Rob put more importance on my relationship with the Lord and being courageous enough to gently rebuke me than in keeping quiet, knowing I might reject him forever because of his decision to speak the truth in love to me. In some strange way, his rebuke made me feel safer than I ever had in any other relationship. Even though I didn't like the confrontation, I knew I wanted a man I could respect more than someone who would let me continue living in ways that displeased God without calling my attention to my sin. When Rob asked me to marry him that December, I, unhesitatingly said yes. Other than my decision to ask Christ to be the Savior and Lord of my life, the decision to become Rob's wife has been the best one I have ever made.

Wounded pride is not a valid reason to withhold forgiveness.

We will begin to see tomorrow how very important Joseph's decision to tell the true interpretations of the two dreams to both officials would be to his future. Sometimes our heart's deepest desire may only be achieved when we do what is most difficult and tell the truth, even when the reward for our obedience is not immediate. We will see this revelation come to life for Joseph in the weeks to come.

Day Five – Remember Me

Some of the happiest memories I have from growing up in Congo were the days when mail was flown into our mission station. Mission Aviation Fellowship (MAF) would take a detour toward Nkara Ewa with a small single engine airplane when my parents could fit the airplane's flight path into a mail drop without having to pay the high cost of chartering the flight. Our shortwave CB radio was the only link of communication we had with the outside world. Mom would learn of the day that the plane was coming and its arrival would be anticipated all week by us. We would count down how many days were left in the week before we would hear from our loved ones who lived 8500 miles away. The actual day the mail came was hardly bearable as we would imagine we could hear the faraway drone of the plane's engine every half hour.

Finally, our imagination would become reality as the drone we thought we were hearing all day would turn out to be real. We would scream with excitement as we climbed aboard the seven-ton 1957 diesel army truck that my parents had purchased. Our station was in a valley while the airstrip was located on one of the three hills that formed a horseshoe around the 280 acre piece of property that made up Nkara Ewa. The three mile trip up the hill would find us singing and shouting and wondering who had remembered us way out in the bush of Congo. Mail could take six weeks or six months to get to us. We did not care how old the news was in the letters. We devoured any news we received from our homeland. We would read each piece of mail (including bulletins from our home church in Michigan) until we had practically memorized each sentence. I would daydream of what my friends were doing while my mouth watered over the dinners my southern grandmother cooked and wrote to tell about.

Long before the days of email or texting, a handwritten note was a treasure to me. Looking back, none of the news in those cherished letters was particularly exciting in its content. What mattered was that someone whom I loved and missed so much had remembered me. I never threw a single letter away in four years.

What is the most cherished letter you have ever received and why?

Let's remind ourselves of the momentous changes in Joseph's life this week. Answer the following questions (without looking back at your study, if you can!):

Where did Joseph find himself after leaving Potiphar's house?

Why did he find himself there?

What did he experience from the Lord in his new location?

Who was in the same place and what caused them to confide in Joseph?

How did Joseph come to their aid?

I love suspense as long as I can know how things are eventually resolved. I used to glance nervously at the clock as I watched my favorite television show with so many loose ends to tie up and only five minutes remaining before the end of the show for the week. We left yesterday's lesson without knowing what was going to be the outcome of Joseph's truthful interpretations of both dreams. The cupbearer had received a favorable interpretation and the baker had been told he was about to lose his head.

I used to avoid the Bible because I was either afraid that I wouldn't be able to understand the verses in its pages or because I thought the stories it contained were boring or irrelevant to my life. I cannot believe how wrong I was about both of those misconceptions. I remember there was a television commercial for a spaghetti sauce with the tag line, "It's all in there." The commercial boasted about all the wonderful ingredients that made this particular sauce the best on the market. Scripture has all the "ingredients" to make these true, ancient stories spring to life in my own circumstances. Drama, adventure, romance, betrayal, cliffhangers, redemption ... these are all in the pages of Scripture.

I used to avoid the Bible because I was either afraid that I wouldn't be able to understand the verses in its pages or because I thought the stories it contained were boring or irrelevant to my life.

I wanted to spend some time today on two verses that we read yesterday, but did not discuss. Let's read Genesis 40:14-15 and answer the following questions:

What did Joseph ask of the cupbearer in verse 14?

Thinking of your own life, has there been a situation in which you pleaded your case to someone you believed could help you in a way that you were unable to help yourself? How helpful was that person to your need?

List the specific facts that Joseph told the cupbearer in verse 15:

Whom did Joseph condemn as he related his unfair circumstances to the cupbearer? Circle the correct answer:

His brothers   Potiphar   Potiphar's wife   No one

Underline those above whom you think Joseph would have been justified in condemning?

My sweet sister, there are some principles in Scripture that are hard for me to swallow and even more difficult to obey. None are more difficult than the commands in which Jesus gave me in how to treat someone who has mistreated me. Record each of the following commands of Scripture regarding our enemies:

Proverbs 24:17:

Proverbs 25:21:

Matthew 5:43-44:

Which of the passages above is most difficult for you right now to obey and why?

The wisdom of God is the attribute whereby He accomplishes the best possible results by the best possible means for the most possible people for the longest time for His greatest glory.

These passages used to make me burn with anger while I remained ignorant of God's character. Why did someone get to mistreat me when I was to be kind in response to their nastiness? Was I just supposed to be a doormat for the ugly behavior that was inflicted on me? That did not sound like justice to me. My anger stemmed from not understanding that God sees everything. Everything. But there are times when, in His perfect wisdom, He remains merciful to the one on whom I want to avenge myself. I heard this quote from a well-known pastor:

The wisdom of God is the attribute whereby He accomplishes the best possible results by the best possible means for the most possible people for the longest time for His greatest glory. [2]

I have mulled that statement over in my mind. I have come to realize that I consider justice served only when I see it happen on my timetable. In my myopic, narrow view of justice, I only want justice for me. My flesh does not care all that God is accomplishing in and through my pain in my life and in others. I just want justice for me right now. My obedience to the Scriptures in Proverbs and Matthew's gospel may never make a bit of sense to me. I may live and die never seeing the justice I desire towards my enemy. But my life touches more people than I can possibly imagine. Perhaps my children will face a life circumstance that requires forgiveness that they absolutely know they are not capable of giving – forgiveness that will save a marriage, enable a parent-child relationship to be restored, or provide grace for a once-destroyed friendship to be healed. Could it be possible that my obedience to treat my enemies like Joseph did – to not slander them or tell the injustices committed to me to anyone who will listen – will continue to reap a harvest of righteousness long after I am gone? The answer is found in Psalm 15.

List the benefits of Psalm 15 and how these benefits are acquired:

Just as Joseph had predicted, three days after each man received God's interpretation of his individual dream, Pharaoh had a royal birthday. Both men were released from prison, but to very different fates.

After reading Genesis 40:20-23, describe what happened to:

The cupbearer (verse 21):

The baker (verse 22):

Joseph (verse 23):

My dear sister, life is full of crushing disappointments as we realize those individuals we put our hope in do not do what they had promised to do. Maybe we wrestle with a parent who continually broke promises to us when we were young and trusting. Maybe we have given our heart to someone of the opposite sex who has been careless and abusive. Perhaps something was stolen from us that we worked so hard for by someone we thought had our best interest at heart.

Why has God allowed these agonies to be part of our lives? The question we must ask ourselves is where were we putting our hope and trust? Do we now realize that instead of trusting in the One who is omniscient, omnipresent, and has the power to change our circumstances, we were trusting in a human being with none of those abilities?

Who did Isaiah come to realize was the person in control of the refining that comes through life's disappointments in Isaiah 48:10-11?

Our God is all about His glory. There is no earthly joy that can touch having a part in His glory. He is such a generous and loving Father. He allows us to come to the end of ourselves so that when His glory is revealed, in due time, we will know, to the core of our beings, that we nor any puny human being had anything to do with the peace, deep contentment, and fulfilling purpose in which we are now a part. He will allow deep pain so that we can clearly hear His voice behind us saying, "This is the way, walk in it," (Isaiah 30:18-21). How destructive our lives will become when we do not understand that our trust can only be secure in God alone – not in a human being who will disappoint us again and again. And for those of us who are wondering if God has seen our pain or if He has forgotten to remember us, let's meditate on this incredible promise:

Our God is all about His glory.

God, how difficult Your thoughts are for me [to comprehend]; how vast their sum is! If I counted them, they would outnumber the grains of sand; when I wake up, I am still with You.

Psalm 139:17-18 (HCSB)

Jesus knows where we are and what time it is, my dear friend. We can cling to this truth while we wait for His sure salvation in our lives.

The Dark Night of the Soul

But no one says, 'Where is God my Maker, who gives songs in the night..
Job 35:10

I grew up in Congo on a remote bush mission station. The only running water we had was in the water in the tin bucket in our hand as we ran up the hill from our twenty-acre lake. Nothing happened when I flipped my room light switch on during the day because we had electricity only when the diesel generator was operating for three hours each night. My father would inform us that he was going to turn off the generator as he walked out of our house down to the small building in which it was located. I knew that I had less than ten minutes to get to my bedroom before the entire house was swallowed up in the darkness of the African night. If there was no moon that particular night, the inky blackness was almost impenetrable.

When my soul feels as though it is in the dark, I can panic and feel desperately alone. I wonder, my dear friend, if you have experienced a season when the presence of God seemed a distant memory or inaccessible. Maybe, like Joseph, we are reeling under the injustice of being falsely accused and are having to bear hardship as a result of someone's negligence or slander. Maybe we are walking through a fog of grief over a loss of someone or something cherished by us.

I am convinced, my precious friend, that God does His deepest work in the dark night of our souls, if we allow Him. If we cling to Jesus, even when we cannot readily see Him in our situation, He will give us songs in the night, which He taught us, that we have never sung before. We will look back at the trial and be able to thank Him for intimate knowledge about our Christ that we did not and could not possess without the darkness. We will trust Him more. If we hold on to His unchanging character, we will understand more fully that He is good, even when our prayers are not answered in the way we had hoped.

This week we will dare to wrestle with questions that we may have been unwilling or afraid to ask of God. We will examine feelings of abandonment, disappointment, anger in our journey with Him as we prepare to witness the irrefutable proof of God's presence in Joseph's life through his stunning deliverance from prison.

God is big enough for our deepest questions. Only He has the power to change the darkest periods in our lives into treasure that cannot be acquired any other way than through the dark night of the soul.

Day 1 – The Abyss of Abandonment

Hot tears coursed down my temples and splashed into my ears. Scenes of a dark room darted between dreams that made no sense to me, deepening my confusion about my whereabouts. One thought was extremely clear to me: I desperately wanted my mother.

I would weakly call out for her through a parched throat, but each time I called and she didn't appear, the terror was reinforced that my need for her comfort was going to be unmet. As I lay there, staring up at the ceiling, I would vaguely remember that reality of the distance between us as the tears would start again.

I was in the seventh grade, six hundred miles away from home at a mission boarding school, and very ill with a sunstroke. The sunstroke allowed only brief times of lucid thoughts not plagued with hallucinations. The comfort I longed for from my mother was inaccessible to me as a dense jungle which could not be traversed by a vehicle prevented her from coming to my side. I felt utterly abandoned and heartsick.

Satan has carefully laid a net down for each of us individually in the form of life's disappointments and unmet expectations to lie to us about the unconditional love that God has for His children.

Name a time in your life when you felt abandoned (e.g. by a friend, a parent, a boyfriend, a spouse) and use three words to describe that emotion:

Psalm 140:5 says: *Proud men have hidden a snare for me; they have spread out the cords of their net and have set traps for me along my path.*

Satan was cast out of heaven with a third of the angels because he wanted to make himself like God (see Isaiah 14:12-17). Pride was at the root of his evil desire. Satan hates those who belong to Jesus Christ with an intense hatred. He is the antithesis of anything that is good. He longs to steal, kill, and destroy all those who believe the lie that God has abandoned them. Satan has carefully laid a net down for each of us individually in the form of life's disappointments and unmet expectations to lie to us about the unconditional love that God has for His children. He is a liar and the father of all lies (John 8:44). He does not speak the truth because he mixes shades of truth with lies. There is no such thing as a half-truth - just a whole lie. A tool Satan continually uses is discouragement against the children of the Most High. He does not want us to know the following truths about God's infinite concern for you and me.

What do the following verses reveal about God toward His own?

Psalm 5:3:

Psalm 17:6:

Psalm 56:8:

Isaiah 63:9:

I wanted us to do the following exercise and glean insight through a comparison of how Joseph reacted to life's cruelty with our own reactions in similar situations. Please answer as honestly as you can.

1) Family or friend's betrayal:

Joseph's reaction	My reaction

2) Forced to submit to Potiphar as a slave (think of how this applies to you):

Joseph's reaction	My reaction

3) Faced with great sexual temptation:

Joseph's reaction	My reaction

4) Falsely accused and punished:

Joseph's reaction	My reaction

5) Choice to serve others while in personal pain:

Joseph's reaction	My reaction

2 Corinthians 4:17-18 reveals the secret to why Joseph was able to react in a God-honoring way to the injustice of each of these situations. What is the secret?

Looking back at the Scripture we looked up together about God's concern for you and then pondering how you reacted in each of these life situations, did you react as you did because you believed the lies of Satan or because you trusted in the character of God even when you could not sense His presence?

We do such a disservice to ourselves and to biblical characters when we falsely believe that someone like Joseph was devoid of human emotions. I have found myself doing this when the biblical text is silent about what the individual felt. I have decided that the person always made the right decision and was somehow free of the emotional baggage that clouds our decisions and thoughts. There was only one perfect Person who ever lived on this earth. His name is Jesus Christ. The book of Hebrews reveals the painful path of suffering that God the Father chose for Christ on earth and the stunning results that followed Christ's obedience.

After reading Hebrews 5:7-10, let's ponder these questions together:

There was only one perfect Person who ever lived on this earth. His name is Jesus Christ.

How did Jesus call out to God during His time on earth (vs. 7):

What does verse 7 say about the One who could save Jesus from death? Fill in the blanks:

"...and [Jesus] was ________ because of His reverent ____________________."

Keep a finger in Hebrews 5, but let's go to Luke 22:39-44 to see this verse come to life. What was about to happen to Christ and what did He do in these verses?

Write out Jesus' words from the cross in Matthew 27:46:

Hebrews 5:7 tells us that Jesus was heard from the cross by the Father whose will it was to have Christ pay the penalty for our sin. But even Jesus felt unheard, abandoned, and alone on the cross. Why? Why would the perfect Son of God who died on a cruel and undeserved death of torture be allowed to feel abandoned by His Father?

What does Hebrews 5:8 tell us that Jesus learned from His suffering?

My darling friend, can we see that Jesus Christ also wanted God to take away the suffering? Although Jesus was fully God, He was also fully man – just like you and me. And it was God's will to crush Him and cause Christ to suffer (Isaiah 53:10). Why? To be cruel, to be heartless, to abandon His beloved Son? No!

What does Hebrews 5:9-10 reveal that the crushing and suffering accomplished in Christ and allows Him to be for us?

Christ's death and suffering did not make Him morally perfect. He was already morally perfect before the cross. But because of the unfathomable love of Christ for a lost world, the only way for Jesus to become perfect in His human experience and be able to empathize with broken sinners was to suffer in His humanity like we do (see Hebrews 5:7-10). When those nails broke His skin, blood gushed from the wound. He knew agony physically on the cross just like some of us have been called to know. And He also experienced the emotional agony of abandonment that Joseph and you and me know.

... the only way for Jesus to become perfect in His human experience and be able to empathize with broken sinners was to suffer in His humanity like we do.

What did Jesus proclaim in front of all who were at the tomb of Lazarus, just before He raised Lazarus from the dead in John 11:41?

Yet, Jesus, in His humanity, screamed out from the cross in the agony of the silence of God. Although God the Father heard Christ's screams and anguish, He did not rescue Him because there was a greater purpose to be accomplished that could not be accomplished any other way than Christ facing the pain of abandonment on the cross. Christ's suffering paid the penalty you and I could never pay caused by our sin. Christ's death and resurrection secured the eternal salvation that God the Father offers to all who come to Him through His Son, Jesus Christ.

Are you in the middle of a hundred pieces of a shattered part of your life, my darling sister? The shattering may have come from someone else or the shattering may have come from our own sinful decisions. It is the broken and contrite heart that Jesus promises He will not despise. Jesus, the Redeemer, who fully knows the deepest anguish and hurt you have suffered, has the ability to take those hundred shards and, with absolute perfect wisdom and power, redesign the mess our lives may have become. There is no throw-away life when the Master of the universe picks up the shattered pieces and makes all things new.

The God who promised He would never leave us or forsake us wants us to believe, by faith, that He has not abandoned us. He longs to be gracious to us and show us His compassion (Isaiah 30:18).

We are hard pressed on every side, but not crushed; perplexed, but not in despair; persecuted, but not abandoned; struck down, but not destroyed. We always carry around in our body the death of Jesus, so that the life of Jesus may also be revealed in our body. ***2 Corinthians 4:8-10***

Knowing the truth changes everything. God had lessons Joseph could not learn anywhere other than in prison walls. As we close, I wanted us to ask the Lord to show us where He was in those painful times when we felt abandoned and how we came to believe the lie that He had forsaken us. God is always at work. We need to ask for eyes to be able to see what He was and is doing in our lives. I am so proud of your obedience!

We need to ask for eyes to be able to see what He was and is doing in our lives.

Day 2 – Angry At God

Have you ever pondered whether you are angry with God about what He has allowed?

I have known since I was a little girl that I could hide nothing from God, but when I look back at my actions, I have come to realize that this knowledge sometimes got lost on the way from my head to my heart. I was deceiving myself into believing that He somehow did not know everything I thought or desired – especially when sin was involved in my actions.

We live in a world in which tolerance is preached from the rooftops. Truth has been sacrificed for the nauseating quagmire of political correctness. As I am writing this lesson, the western world is rejoicing over the killing of the mastermind behind the horrific events of September 11, 2001, when 3000 innocent civilians lost their lives in the World Trade Center in the heart of New York City. Most see the death of this wicked man as justice served. Every human being, no matter how fervently he or she believes in the rights of human beings to live as they please, has an inner moral compass that says that the killing of innocent human lives deserves punishment.

We live in a world in which tolerance is preached from the rooftops.

What accounts for this call to justice that each of us innately possesses regarding life's unfair treatment of us or those we love? Let's look up the following Scriptures to discover the answer to these questions:

Genesis 1:27 tell us that human beings are made in __________ ____________.

Isaiah 30:18 tells us that the Lord is a God of ______________________.

2 Chronicles 19:7 says that with God there is no ______________________ or ______________________ or ______________________.

Isaiah 13:11 declares that God Himself will _______________ the world for its __________, the wicked for their _____________.

Every person, whether he or she recognizes the truth of Scripture, was created in the image of God. We long for justice because God is a God of justice. We long for equal treatment by others because God shows no partiality. And when someone has committed an action that we believe is punishable, we want to see vengeance on the offender. Why? Because all of those emotions are part of the character of God.

But what happens when we do not see the justice of God in our situations? What happens when we are sitting in a prison cell emotionally and the door has clanged shut because of someone else's actions toward us? The bars are impenetrable. Our freedom is gone because our thoughts are consumed with the injustice of what has happened to us. Even more grievous is the fact that our perpetrator seems to be walking around free in the sunshine while we sit in the darkness.

After reading Psalm 73:3-14, which of his complaints do you resonate with when you think of the one(s) you are struggling to forgive?

Do you wrestle with obeying James 2:12-13? What do these verses command us to do?

I am going to be gut-level honest. There are some days that I long for God's vengeance to triumph over His mercy towards those I judge not to be deserving of that mercy.

There are some days that I long for God's vengeance to triumph over His mercy towards those I judge not to be deserving of that mercy.

Imagine Joseph's life story was your own. Rate in order whom it would be hardest to show mercy to from the following list and include your reasons why:

___ Joseph's brothers:

___ Potiphar:

___ Potiphar's wife:

___ The cupbearer:

Do you believe that Joseph struggled in prison with thoughts of revenge toward his brothers? Scripture is silent about this, but explain the reason for your answer.

Many people, even those who never attended church growing up, are familiar with the story of the prophet Jonah who was swallowed by a big fish (there is no mention of a "whale" in the story) and lived to tell about the experience. But many do not go on to read the rest of this profound book in Scripture. Jonah was sent to preach a message of repentance to some of the most feared enemies of his homeland, Israel.

The Assyrians were known as some of the most barbaric people who ever lived. They would skin people alive and then impale them on sharpened stakes and abandon them to die a slow, torturous death. The Ninevites, people who lived in the capital city of Assyria, would bury their conquered enemies up to their necks in sand and leave them to die in the elements without food and water or to the ravaging hunger of wild animals.[1]

Jonah decided he would buy a one way ticket to Tarshish for a sea voyage that would take him as far away from Ninevah as he could get. A terrible storm ensued because of Jonah's disobedience. The crew of the ship was forced to throw him into the sea after they had unsuccessfully begged Jonah's God to forgive them for their actions. Rather than drowning, Jonah was in a prison of his own in the belly of a fish, which finally vomited Jonah onto dry land after three days. Jonah then reluctantly decided to obey God and go to Ninevah to preach a message of repentance to his hated enemies.

After reading Jonah 3:1-10 and Jonah 4:1-2, how did Jonah react to God's decision to relent and show mercy to his hated enemies in Jonah 4:2?

To put this story in a context we can understand, what God asked Jonah to do would be like Him asking someone who had lost a loved one in one of the twin towers of the World Trade Center on September 11, 2001 to go preach a message of repentance to the families of the hijackers in order to turn His wrath away from them. Can we understand how, humanly speaking, Jonah burned with anger at the seeming injustice of God as He relented and turned away His wrath from the Ninevites?

What did Jonah want God to do to him in Jonah 4:3?

My darling sister, can you and I relate to Jonah's anguish and fury? Does the thought of God extending mercy to the one who has hurt you deeply, the one who you cannot yet forgive, make you exceedingly angry? I love that Scripture is honest with us. Jonah was a righteous man! He knew God! He loved Jehovah. But Jonah was a human being just like you and me. He was furious with God's decision to be merciful to the Ninevites, whom he believed deserved the full wrath of God. If I am brutally honest, my heart feels empathy with Jonah's distress over God's mercy toward those whom I don't believe deserve His kindness.

What was God's response to Jonah in Jonah 4:4?

What would you say in response to the Holy Spirit asking you the same question?

How did Jonah respond to God's question in verse 5? He ignored God. He decided to sit down and pout on the outskirts of Nineveh, hoping to see God rain down fire and brimstone that would destroy the city.

Let's continue to read Jonah 4:5-11.

What made Jonah very happy in verse 6? Underline the correct response:

A cooling vine
A plague fell on the city
A fire that fell from heaven

What happened in verse 8 and how did Jonah respond to God?

Never before or since has there been a revival recorded where an entire city, taking three days to walk through, was confronted with the message of repentance and turned toward God like Nineveh did. And instead of being thankful that those who had been enemies of God had been reconciled to Jehovah, Jonah wanted them to die and face an eternity without the Redeemer, never knowing His mercy.

Are you and I just waiting for God to lower the boom on the ones who have hurt us so deeply? Are we sulking and seething over His mercy toward them? Are we more joyful over a material possession that has no soul than over the possibility that God could reconcile our perpetrator to Himself and work in that person's life to bring Him glory?

The gospel of Matthew records a time when Jesus told His disciples about a servant who owed his master a debt he could not possibly pay back in his lifetime. After the servant threw himself down at the feet of his master and begged forgiveness for the debt, the master graciously forgave the servant of all he owed him. Soon after, the master was informed that the same servant he had forgiven had thrown a fellow servant in prison who owed the forgiven servant a much smaller amount. The master was so outraged by the ingratitude of the servant he had forgiven that the master ordered the merciless servant to be tortured in prison until he paid back all he had originally owed.

What chilling words did Jesus say about God's reaction to our unforgiveness toward others in Matthew 18:35?

What were we once called by God according to Colossians 1:21?

How did He show us His mercy according to Colossians 1:22?

After reading Titus 3:3-7, what were we guilty of according to verse 3?
Why were we rescued according to verses 4-5?

How lavishly have we been forgiven according to verse 6-7?

We want our perpetrator to be tortured, but, when we refuse to forgive, aren't we actually the ones suffering the greatest torture with our obsessive anger, bitterness, and the insatiable need we have for revenge toward the one who betrayed us, slandered us, or stole something precious from us? How much have we been robbed of joy, purpose, and the abundant life Jesus promised us in John 10:10 because we, who deserve hell for our great sins against God, have refused to forgive someone who owes us so much less than we owe our Savior, Jesus Christ?

I believe with all of my heart that Joseph struggled with thoughts of vengeance toward his brothers. I believe that his heart struggled to comprehend how prison in a land in which he was a foreigner was justice for him when his brothers were walking free at home with their father, Jacob. But I also believe with all my heart that God's deepest work in Joseph was accomplished in the darkness of that dungeon. Because, you see, God had a purpose for Joseph that was bigger than he could possibly imagine – the saving of an entire family, including those brothers that betrayed him at the deepest level, who would have surely been wiped out by the famine that was looming in the near future. Although Christ's birth would not occur for many centuries after Joseph, Jacob's family (through the line of Judah) would bring forth the Messiah, Jesus Christ, who would be the Savior of any that would seek Him. Joseph's decision to forgive still affects you and me today. How our decision to forgive will affect the world remains to be seen, but we can rest on the promise our righteous Judge, who will call every person to account for what he or she has done, makes about Himself:

The sins we have examined in our families in the first weeks of this study will continue to the next generation until someone stands with God and says, "Enough! I choose to forgive by Your strength because I cannot do it on my own!

I make known the end from the beginning,
from ancient times, what is still to come.
I say: My purpose will stand,
and I will do all that I please.
Isaiah 46:10

We can choose to be part of a purpose that will blow our minds. A purpose that has the power to redeem, restore, and reconcile the wrong that has been done to us. A purpose that will affect not just us, but generations to come. Or we can choose a legacy of bitterness and anger. The sins we have examined in our families in the first weeks of this study will continue to the next generation until someone stands with God and says, "Enough! I choose to forgive by Your strength because I cannot do it on my own! Jesus, help me!"

As we leave today's lesson, may the Holy Spirit have the freedom to ask us the same question the Lord asked of Jonah:

But the LORD replied, "Have you any right to be angry?"

Day 3 – To Remove the Blindness of Disappointment

I have an NIV study Bible which I have received from my parents while I was a college student. I smile every time I come across the passage of Matthew 7:7, which reads:

Ask and it will be given to you; seek and you will find; knock and the door will be opened to you.

There is a date written next to that passage and a name of a young man that I was asking God to let me marry twenty years ago. I could think of no valid reason why I shouldn't be able to marry him. I had made a list of the qualities I had wanted in a husband and, with the exception of one or two more insignificant qualities, he epitomized my dream life partner. I felt confident that a relationship with him would be fully in line with God's will.

As I look back in my journal over the months of the wrenching emotional roller-coaster ride I was on of begging God for someone I thought was best for me, I am now able to see the heights of exhilaration and despair that I alternated between. On paper, we would have been perfect together. This young man had shown interest in me first. My hopes were not altogether unfounded. Page after page of my journal recorded my increasing desperation, along with the bitterness of my disappointment, as the truth slowly sank in that this relationship was not going to happen. I cried a river of tears into my pillow many nights over my shattered dream. It was one of the most difficult times of my young adult life.

Disappointment can become the womb of bitterness and resentment.

I believe that one of the most difficult challenges we face as believers in Jesus Christ is coming face to face with the fact that God does not shield us from disappointment. Disappointment can become the womb of bitterness and resentment. When I look back at some of the darkest times in my life, disappointment looms large.

What does Hebrews 12:14-15 reveal about the danger of staying in the bitterness of our disappointment?

Bitterness is like a whip. It will relentlessly beat us until we are deformed and scarred. The most damaging consequence of bitterness is our blindness to see the Lord in our circumstances.

What do the following passages of Scripture reveal about God's intimate knowledge of us from Psalm 139?

verse 1:

verse 3:

verses 11-12:

verses 16-18:

As Joseph continued his time in prison with no hope of a better life, he must have had time to reflect on how different his life had been with his father, Jacob, before he was sold as a slave to Potiphar.

What might have Joseph been trusting in before he came to Egypt? Check all that you think apply:

His father's love
His family position
The multi-colored coat given by Jacob.

Which one of the securities above that he might have trusted in before being sold to Egypt could help him in prison? Not one.

For I know the plans I have for you," declares the LORD, "plans to prosper you and not to harm you, plans to give you hope and a future.

Now it's your turn. Thinking about your own disappointment, were you trusting in someone or something of this earth (a job, your family, a spouse, a child, a friend, a bank account) to give you a false sense of security? Share your thoughts:

So why does the Lord allow profound disappointment in the life of one of His beloved children? Jeremiah 29:11 boldly says, ***For I know the plans I have for you," declares the LORD, "plans to prosper you and not to harm you, plans to give you hope and a future.***

How can we reconcile disappointment being part of the good plans and purposes that God has for each one of us? We are going to spend the rest of our study in God's magnificent Word today with two men who found themselves asking that very question.

Turn to Luke 24. Let's read verses 1-11 and make several observations together:

Whose tomb was being visited and by whom?

What was the astonishing news the women heard and from whom (verses 4-6)?

Whom did the women tell and what was the reaction of those they told (verse 11)?

Have you remembered being told something would occur only after the event happened? When circumstances unfold in front of you, only then do you understand that somehow the details of what you had been told had slipped your mind or you realize that you did not fully comprehend what you were being told until after the event had occurred. I have never known anyone personally who has been raised from the dead. Neither had these women. Imagine the profound shock and exhilaration they must have felt as the angel helped bring to their memory that Jesus had told them He would die and then be raised to life again.

Let's continue reading Luke 24:13-35.

These two men were not part of the eleven disciples of Jesus as had been mentioned in verse nine, but we have evidence that they were intimate friends and companions of Christ. They surely had seen the miraculous healings He had performed and may have been among the crowd of five thousand fed by Jesus with five loaves of bread and two fish. These men would have been eye-witnesses to Christ's power and hearers of His profound teachings.

We humans process trauma in a healthier way when there is a compassionate and willing ear listening to us.

Despite all of this first-hand contact with Christ, what were they kept from understanding in verses 15-16?

What were they asked by their unknown companion in verses 17 and 19 and what was their emotional state and response?

Did Jesus know what they were about to say? Absolutely. He did not ask that question to be given knowledge He did not already possess, but He wanted these two men to verbalize their sorrow. We humans process trauma in a healthier way when there is a compassionate and willing ear listening to us.

How often do you follow the example of the writer of Psalm 142:1-2 concerning what has disappointed you? Check the best answer:

______ Always ______ Often ______ Rarely ______ Never

Whom do you generally pour your heart out to? Circle all that apply:

Spouse Best friend Parent Co-worker Sibling
No one

Can any of these persons change your situation? If your answer is no, consider your reasons for sharing your hurt with your choice(s):

Write out phrases in verses 19-24 that speak of the men's profound disappointment. Note anything that leads you to believe they were struggling with doubt over Jesus being the Son of God, whom He claimed to be many times.

What rebuke did Jesus give the men in verse 26?

I have sat under some gifted Bible study teachers since the day thirteen years ago on my family room floor when I begged Jesus to make Himself real to me. But I truly cannot, in my wildest dreams, imagine the teaching that must have taken place on the road with Jesus explaining all of Scripture to these sorrowing men.

Are we disappointed with Jesus and is that disappointment based on our own unmet expectations of who we think He should be or on Scriptural truth?

Did the Bible study they had together make them realize who He was while they were walking together? No. The Son of God Himself, the Man these two men had devoted the last three years of their lives to follow, had been walking with them for hours. They had expected Jesus to fulfill their own expectations of what His role in their lives would be. Their expectations were not based on Scripture or they would have been able to recognize the truth. And my eyes fill with tears because I realize that I am guilty of the same blindness as these dearly loved followers of the Savior of the world were. I ask the next question with absolutely no condemnation, but tender empathy:

Are we disappointed with Jesus and is that disappointment based on our own unmet expectations of who we think He should be or on Scriptural truth?

Life has not turned out as we expected. Have we missed Him all along because we are busy pouring out our complaint to someone who cannot do anything about our pain other than being a sounding board? Has bitterness taken root so that we cannot see the Lord? If I cannot see Him in the darkness of my life, it is not because He has not been there. It is because of my own limited understanding of the grand purpose that my disappointment will play in a pivotal role that will bring Him much glory.

What specific act did Jesus perform when the men finally recognized Him (vv. 30-31)?

Not until the two men sat across the table with Jesus were their eyes opened when He broke the bread. How many times in the last three years had they watched Him, as their beloved Friend and Teacher, do that simple, yet profoundly intimate act? Bible study will mean nothing to you and me if Jesus remains a second, third, or last alternative for comfort when we are sitting in the darkness of life's disappointments. Do we trust Him?

In that moment, they understood that the plan in which they had been so disappointed was actually the pathway of hope. Not until their own plans were dashed, not until their own false securities were taken away, not until they were left with nothing, were they able to see that what they had believed to be profound disappointment was the pathway to glory. Their myopic vision had not been able to grasp the truth. Jesus had been faithful all along to them. He has been faithful to you and me also.

The LORD himself goes before you and will be with you; he will never leave you nor forsake you. Do not be afraid; do not be discouraged.
– Deuteronomy 31:8

Joseph had no way of knowing how profoundly his life was about to change after God allowed such horrible disappointment to be part of his experience. The dizzying heights of power God had prepared for Joseph would have been treacherous had he not been weaned from the sham of earth's puny securities. Disappointment had to come before honor for Joseph. What honor awaits us if we believe that the Lord Himself, who goes before us, has never left us or forsaken us?

The dizzying heights of power God had prepared for Joseph would have been treacherous had he not been weaned from the sham of earth's puny securities.

Day Four – The Hardest Lesson to Learn

I was obsessed with one thought – moving to Nashville, Tennessee. Two of my siblings had made the move from Detroit many years before to follow their dreams of a music career. My sister had recently married and moved to Chicago, and while I would be moving away from my parents and youngest brother and his family, Nashville was where my other brother was still living. I became addicted to house listing websites that showed my future dream house. I ate, breathed, and dreamed the months away logged onto realtor websites while I impatiently wondered why God hadn't already moved us. I penned in my journal that I did not understand what God was trying to teach me. *What could I possibly learn of value as I had to wait over saying goodbye to harsh winters and the higher cost of living in my home state,* I wondered?

What do you do when you are waiting for something you have become impatient for? Circle all that apply:

Become depressed — Forget to live in the present
Study my Bible more — Call out to God
Become stressed — Become controlling
Turn to addictions (internet, TV, overeating, undereating)

What does Psalm 46:10 tell us to do? What does this specifically look like right now in your struggle to forgive?

We each have our own idea of what justice looks like in our situations. Has what has happened to us been in vain if we never see the justice we were hoping for come to pass to the person who hurt us? What would be the purpose of those greatest moments of pain and agony we have suffered if we never see anything tangibly changing between us and the person who has wounded us?

What does Isaiah 45:7 reveal to us about God that we might not have realized?

What did Job say in reply to his wife after they had lost every one of their ten children and all of their material possessions in Job 2:9-10?

There is a side of God that we do not hear about much anymore. Because we are unaware of our deep and unmet hunger, many of us are starving for the full counsel of God. Many of our churches stay away from teaching that God has a side to Him that should fill us with holy fear. This is not just fear that inspires us with wonder as we stand at the edge of some magnificent masterpiece in nature (like the Grand Canyon in Utah), but the kind of fear that understands that we should tremble at the power that God holds to blow away His enemies with the breath of His nostrils. Isaiah was terrified when he saw the Lord in the temple and said, *"Woe to me! I am ruined! For I am a man of unclean lips and I live among a people of unclean lips, and my eyes have seen the King, the Lord Almighty (Isaiah 6:5).*

God has allowed what has happened to you and me. Let me repeat that statement again. God has allowed what has happened to you and me. Without the empowering Word of God to set us free from the prison of bitterness that this realization brings, we are doomed to continue to be in bondage to the one(s) we are struggling to forgive.

What benefit can possibly come from learning to wait? Why did God allow Joseph to be sold as a slave by his own flesh and blood, falsely accused of rape by a woman against whom he could not defend himself, and be forgotten by a fellow prisoner who was set free while Joseph stayed in his cell? What lessons are so valuable that cannot be learned unless immense pain is involved?

I cannot possibly answer those questions adequately. But what I do have access to is the character of God. I must absolutely believe the following truths about who God is and what His heart is toward me or I will wither and die emotionally and spiritually under the pain that is lived out during the dark night of the soul.

God has allowed what has happened to you and me.

Paraphrase what the following Scriptures reveal about God's purpose for pain in our lives:

Job 5:17:

Proverbs 11:21:

Isaiah 30:18-21:

Isaiah 54:16-17:

Isaiah 61:1-4:

One of the most quoted Scriptures is Romans 8:28. Write out the verse here:

We too often stop with that verse. Now let's read Romans 8:29-30.

Romans 8:29-30 gives us the how behind Romans 8:28, which is to conform me to the likeness of His Son, Jesus Christ. I don't want to fully understand how God uses **all** things for my good. I would prefer to be ignorant of those circumstances and relationships that cause me to be uncomfortable and force me to reevaluate my life and my attitudes and actions that are not Christ-honoring. My sinful nature wants Him to use comfort, leisure, and my fleshly desires to make me more like Christ. I do not want to have to look at my own junk and my contribution to the mess I may find myself, including my own bitterness, hatred, and ability to bear a grudge. I never have a day when I wake up and do not sin against God in some way. I never have a day of total victory when every thought I think is pure and Christ-honoring. Ask my children about the impatience, unkindness, and selfishness that comes pouring out of my mouth. My husband knows that I struggle to put his interests above my own. As long as I am in this body that is decaying each year with a heart that does what the Holy Spirit hates (see Romans 7:14-19), ***I will not change unless I am forced to do so.*** Pain allows me to hear the voice of my teacher behind me so that I can clearly know which way I should go to leave my pain behind.

I will not change unless I am forced to do so.

What is the purpose of our lives, my dear sisters? I just spent a few days on one of the most luxurious places I have ever visited. The island boasts a gated community which has six championship golf courses (my husband's idea of utopia). The weather is spectacular for ten months out of the year. The lawns are immaculately groomed. No dirt. No mess. My daughters and I went down to one of the two marinas to look for seashells. As the delicious breeze wafted in from the ocean, I was tempted to forget the starkness of the living situation of people outside the gates. Many are desperately poor and without hope. Just a few miles outside the gate we went through to go into the city, we passed a homeless woman with unkempt hair wearing a profoundly sad expression as she sat on a bus stop bench.

My flesh loves comfort, leisure, and to forget that God is more concerned with my holiness than my happiness. Happiness is circumstantial. I can work so hard to make this earth mean to me what only heaven should. I can selfishly think I am owed a life with no pain. I easily become lulled into thinking I am entitled to a life having no storms or white-knuckle moments when I have to throw myself at the feet of the only One who can save me and give me peace that defies explanation in the midst of what I don't fully understand.

My Jesus was a Man of sorrows and acquainted with grief. He never had a home to call His own. He was rejected by His own family members. He was betrayed by one of His twelve most intimate friends. He was misunderstood and slandered. He became weary and exhausted over the demands placed on Him by others. He wept over the death of His dear friend, Lazarus. He was deserted by His friends in His loneliest hours. He felt abandoned by God Himself on the cross. He died a death He did not deserve.

After reading Isaiah 53:10-12, answer the following questions:

Whose will was it that Jesus was crushed and made to suffer?

What would Christ see after the suffering of His soul and because of His knowledge of suffering what would be accomplished for you and me (verse 11)?

What was Christ promised as a reward for the suffering He endured (verse 12)?

What does 2 Corinthians 1:3-5 tell us that we are able to share with others because of our own suffering?

What is the purpose of our suffering according to Job 5:17-18? Contrast this with why human beings wound each other.

We are caught in between the now and the not yet.

Your story and mine are still being written. We do not have the benefit of knowing what the future holds. We are caught in between the now and the not yet. We face the supreme temptation to try to avenge ourselves without ever realizing the wonderful purpose of our pain. The nineteenth-century theologian, Charles Spurgeon, said this:

In prison Joseph learned to wait: I do not know a harder or more valuable lesson. It is worth while to suffer slander and to feel the fret of fetters to acquire the patience which sits still and knows that Jehovah is God...It is amazing how rich and increased in goods we are till the Lord deals with us by a trial, and then full often we discover that we are naked, and poor, and miserable in the very respects in which we boasted about ourselves.[2]

Only God knew, while Joseph languished in prison, to what great heights He was soon going to exalt Joseph. The benefit of learning to wait is that we learn to trust in God's timing. We learn to loosen the death grip of control over our circumstances and relinquish our wills to the One who delights to take into His confidence the upright. Through suffering, we come to realize that we absolutely never had any control over our lives. Only Jesus knows how the very suffering we have gone through will lead us to the abundant life He has promised is ours.

What astounding work does suffering accomplish in us according to 1 Peter 4:1-2?

It is through the hard work of waiting during the dark night of the soul – when we come to the realization that the broken pathway that God has led us on was not just a way, but the best way to conform us into the image of His Son – that we learn the benefits of suffering and can begin to see that the time we are waiting on God has eternal benefits we never realized before.

It was good for me to be afflicted so that I might learn your decrees ... I know, LORD, that your laws are righteous, and that in faithfulness you have afflicted me.

Psalm 119:71, 75

As we close, I wanted us to evaluate our own perspective about our pain through the above verses from Psalm 119. Has our suffering been only suffering with no redeeming value because we didn't know its God-ordained purpose? Would we be willing to ask Him to help us see our suffering through new eyes by what He has revealed to us today through His Word? Share your heart with our faithful God about this.

Day Five – Tried By His Word

The summer of my junior year in high school, we invited fifteen other missionary children to our bush mission station. My dad promised my sister and me that he would create a zip line that would span the width of our twenty-acre lake at the bottom of the hill on which our home was located. I did not know how he was going to make this a reality because my mind did not think mechanically, but I never doubted that he would accomplish this for us and our friends. He worked all through the blistering African heat of the morning and into the early afternoon.

About four o'clock, as the intensity of the day was starting to fade, my father called all of us kids to try out what he had been working on the whole day. We screamed with laughter and delight as we took turns grabbing the handle that ran along the wire strung across the lake and competed to see who would go the farthest before falling into the refreshing water below. I was so proud of my dad and the compliments I heard from my peers over what he had done for us. Many of my friends were surprised that my father would put so much time and effort into something children would enjoy. I was not surprised at all. If my dad made a promise to me, I knew he would do all in his power to fulfill that promise, no matter what the cost to himself. I learned I could count on whatever he promised to happen.

How do you know that someone will keep his or her promise to you? Underline the best answer:

He/she does what was promised.
He/she talks about what he/she will do.

We don't say someone is trustworthy unless we experience that this is true through the evidence of the results of what was promised.

We don't say someone is trustworthy unless we experience that this is true through the evidence of the results of what was promised. We know that someone is not a gossip because we do not have our secret, told in confidence, come back to us through the lips of another person. We know that someone is not a liar because we have seen or heard what was said is the truth.

List a real-life experience to finish the following sentences:

I know that God is trustworthy because...

I know that God does not lie because...

I know that God's Word is true because...

Did you have to think really hard to complete those sentences above, or did the answers come easily? Did what you wrote down happen a long time ago or could you recount a recent (within the last six months) experience to complete the sentences? If our real-life experience happened recently, it may be easier for us to believe that God will be faithful to us again than if the time we last remember seeing Him work in the above ways has becoming a distant memory.

Pick *two* of the following stories in Scripture and describe the real-life experience each person had with God's power in their lives.

2 Kings 4:1-7　　2 Kings 4:8-37　　2 Chronicles 20:5,10-30
Daniel 3:1-30

Answer the following questions:

What impossible situation did this person(s) face without divine intervention?
1)

2)

How did God show His miraculous power in the person's life?
1)

2)

What were the results for the person(s) and/or others who saw the miracle?
1)

2)

Names of God: *Deliverer, Provider, Warrior* or *Healer*

Of the names of God listed above, which one best describes the passages you studied?
1)

2)

Which of the two would have convinced you for all time that God was real and could do what He said He could do? Why?

My dear sisters, what does Isaiah 45:3 tell us is the purpose for the dark night of the soul? Circle the correct answer(s):

To abandon us   To punish us   To know that God is God.

To give us riches in the secret places

Have you been able to see the waiting period He has had you in this way?

We will not understand what the purpose of the darkness was until we look at the treasures God has given us in the dark.

We will not understand what the purpose of the darkness was until we look at the treasures God has given us in the dark. Are we more desperate for Him? Has He shown Himself to be our Provider, our Healer, our Redeemer, the One who fights for us? If you can answer yes to those questions, then the purpose of the darkness has been accomplished!

Without being stripped of the multi-colored coat his father had given him, he may never have learned that material possessions were not where his value was found.

Without the darkness of betrayal, Joseph might have never understood that Jehovah, his God, was the only One on whose love he could depend on. Without facing the injustice of being sold as a slave and being falsely accused, Joseph may never have been willing to serve others in his own pain.

Listen to what Charles Spurgeon has to say about the dungeon God places His beloved children in:

You may rest assured, brethren, that wherever God gives extraordinary gifts or graces, and appoints an extraordinary career, He also appoints unusual trial ... For Joseph to become prime minister of Egypt the path lay through the prison-house: to true honor the road is difficult. Expect, then dear friend, if God gifts thee, or if He graces thee, that He intends to try thee...Every good man is not only tested by trial, but is the better for it. [3]

In all the passages of Scripture we studied in this lesson, each of the persons involved ran directly into their utter helplessness to change their situations. Each one faced their stunning inability to help themselves. There was no place for self-reliance, pride, or the false belief that anything of this world could save them. But they would never have known those life-transforming truths if they had not been forced to go through the experience God had ordained for them! Our darkest moments can be the deepest times of growth when we realize that in our darkness, our God did what He said He would in Scripture!

What is the definition of faith according to Hebrews 11:1? Write out the verse and underline the words *see, certain* and *hope*.

How does 2 Corinthians 5:7 say we are to live?

The darkness forces us to wrestle with God. The darkness forces us to bring our issues of abandonment, our deep disappointment, and anger over what has happened to us to the only One who can heal us in those areas. It allows us to plunder the enemy of our souls as we learn to trust in God's character when we cannot see what He is doing with our natural eyes. The darkness prunes us. It causes us to see what is important in a way we are not able to when we are walking in the sunshine.

The darkness forces us to bring our issues of abandonment, our deep disappointment, and anger over what has happened to us to the only One who can heal us in those areas.

I will rejoice and be glad in your loving kindness, Because You have seen my affliction; you have known the troubles of my soul, And You have not given me over into the hand of the enemy; you have set my feet in a large place.
– Psalm 31:7-8 (NASB)

We need women of God who can testify to the power of the enemy defeated. We need women of God who have experienced miraculous healing of their family members. We need women of God who have walked through the fire and have not been burned. We need women of God who have seen miraculous provision from the God who owns the cattle on a thousand hills. Why? Because we have a dying world who needs to hear about the power of the God who wants to rescue them from a life of despair and a Christ-less eternity.

Are you and I going to trust that the purpose of the darkness that we have experienced in our past or are currently experiencing is not to kill us, but to refine us? Are we going to believe that what has happened to us will result in praise, glory and honor when Jesus Christ is revealed? And do we believe that we are receiving the goal of our faith that is being tested even now, the salvation of our souls?

Only God can redeem the very experiences we were sure would be the end of us. Only He can bring our greatest ministry to others out of the most shattered parts of our hearts that have been miraculously healed through His Word.

"Forget the former things;
do not dwell on the past.
See, I am doing a new thing!
Now it springs up; do you not perceive it?
I am making a way in the desert
and streams in the wasteland.
The wild animals honor me,
the jackals and the owls,
because I provide water in the desert
and streams in the wasteland,
to give drink to my people, my chosen,
the people I formed for myself
that they may proclaim my praise.
– Isaiah 18-21

Has God begun to show you a new way of serving Him that your pain has uniquely qualified you to share with others? Describe your thoughts here:

Only God can redeem the very experiences we were sure would be the end of us.

We are about to see what God had been preparing for Joseph during the thirteen years he spent as a slave and then prisoner. Don't you wish that we could see what God has been doing in us through the very situation that caused us to look for answers about how to forgive in the first place? My dear sister, will you join me in looking expectedly to the One who is doing a new thing in our lives, too, even though we cannot see what it is yet? I pray that we will!

WEEK SIX

High Places

There is an irony that I have found regarding suffering in my walk with Christ. The psalmists, again and again, refer to times of suffering as valley experiences. I will be honest - I dread the valleys! I prefer the sunshine and mountain-tops when all is comfortable and easy in my walk with Christ. I have perceived the valley to be a low place filled with grief, suffering, overwhelming responsibility, or trouble. However, as I have made slow, and sometimes, painful progress, I have come to understand that the valley is not a low place, but rather a high place in which I held fast to Him resulting in greater intimacy in my relationship with Him.

Joseph shared his suffering with the cupbearer. Scripture then shared with us the heartbreaking truth that we have also experienced with others: Joseph was forgotten. It seemed that Joseph's last chance for release from the injustice of the prison was gone forever. Maybe we have never been held prisoners, but we surely can relate to dashed hopes. Tragically, we can come to believe the lie that we, too, have been forgotten.

My dear sister, our God has not forgotten about you and me. Listen to His promise to us while we may be walking through the valley right now:

The steps of a [good] man are directed and established by the Lord when He delights in his way [and He busies Himself with his every step].
Psalm 37:23 (AMP)

This week we are going to see the stunning ways in which God busied Himself with Joseph's every step throughout his suffering. We are going to witness a heart-stopping reunion between Joseph and the brothers who betrayed him. Did Joseph choose to take revenge on the ones who sent him to a living death as a slave away from the father he dearly loved?

Take courage, my sweet friend! God is as intimately involved in our lives as He was in Joseph's deep trouble. Despite our inability to understand what He is doing in our lives, we must praise our Redeemer, Jesus Christ, for His power to make our valleys of trouble into high places of wonder over what He has done in and for us.

Day 1 – When the Impossible Becomes Reality

I could scarcely believe what I was looking at: a positive pregnancy test that informed me that my first child would be arriving in eight months. I had gone through a devastating miscarriage a few months before. With a fragile hope and a great amount of fear, I dared to begin to dream a little that my desire to be a mother would be realized this time. It was early spring in Chicago where I lived and small green buds on the trees were getting ready to burst open. I quickly calculated in my head the season that I would be experiencing when my baby was born. The world would be covered in white, in the deepest part of winter's fierce grip. As I felt spring's warm sun, January seemed very far away. The wait seemed interminable until I could see my newborn's face.

How thankful I am that my son did not arrive until four days before his due date. Every month that he remained in my womb helped him to enter the world as a strong, healthy infant. Although I longed to hold him in my arms from the earliest stages of my pregnancy, I knew that his premature appearance would be a far worse struggle with all of the complications that would be part of a premature birth. When I brought his satiny soft cheeks up to my face to kiss, I did not begrudge any of the days that I had to wait for him to appear.

My dear sister, God has appointed times for you and me to wait. While we are in the wait, we can wonder if there could be any good purpose for the delay. We cannot see God working in any way that is tangible to us.

My dear sister, God has appointed times for you and me to wait.

For what time was the revelation given in Habakkuk 2:3 and how timely would its arrival be?

What does Acts 17:26 reveal about where we are right now in our lives?

If you and I are wondering if God knows where we are or if He has forgotten us, we can be assured in Scripture that those are our own misconceptions of who He is. God knows our exact location and has appointed us to be right where we are at this very moment.

How do we know that God is continuing to work, even when we cannot see any evidence of that truth according to John 5:17?

God's Word never lies to us. He knows exactly where we are and how long we are going to be there and for what purpose. I mistakenly believe that if I don't see tangible results for what I am waiting for, nothing is changing. We live in a culture that declares that success is defined by results. If we can't measure change by the definition we were hoping for, we can assume that nothing is happening in our situations. We may despise the quiet work that is going on in our hearts because it demands us to be still and know that He is God.

Instead of longing for our circumstances to change, what kind of transformation should we be giving ourselves to in our lives according to 2 Corinthians 3:18?

Being transformed into the image of Christ takes a lifetime of walking with Him. It takes faithful days of submitting to His will, even when we cannot fully see the reasons why He wants us to submit. If our wait is producing Christ-likeness in us, then God is surely doing a great work in our lives. He can change our circumstances in a blink of an eye. What we have been waiting for could be given to us tomorrow. Only He knows if the transformation in us into Christ's likeness, which the wait was appointed for, is complete. Has the wait made us rely more fully on God? Has He revealed sin that has to be confessed and turned away from? Have we seen that we are completely helpless without His strength? Have we become more compassionate with others' difficulties because of having to walk in the dark right now? If we are waiting on Him and not rebelling, this quiet time of not seeing the results we were hoping for is doing a great work in us that we will not regret when we look back later.

What are you longing for that you cannot see right now? What blessings or godly changes have been the result of the wait that you might have overlooked?

It is my greatest desire to see women fall in love with Jesus Christ and His Word. I pray that this study would not just be a series of filling in blanks or writing down answers, but that the Spirit of God would have freedom to do a mighty work in our lives. I want us to understand that the God of the universe who worked in Abraham, Isaac, Jacob, and Joseph's lives is the One who longs to have an intimate relationship with you and me. He wants to speak to us, to move in miraculous ways, and redeem our pain so that He is glorified and we are lifted from the pit. There is no hurtful situation that cannot be used in our lives for good.

What was the apostle Paul able to say while he was a prisoner in chains in Philippians 1:19? Are you starting to see hope in your situation that you were unable to see before? Please share here:

We never know when our deliverance will come, but the deliverance we are going to see in Joseph's life today is staggering. To begin our study today, let's read Genesis 41:1-7. Under each column write the dreams' similarities and differences:

Cows out of Nile	Stalks of grain

The last time I checked, cows chew their cud, not their own kind, and stalks of grain do not eat each other. If you and I had a similar set of dreams, we could possibly blame their bizarre contents on a midnight snack we had eaten right before bed. But in the ancient world, dreams were believed to have great meaning. We have to remember that Joseph lived before the first five books of the Bible had been written. You and I have the entire revealed Word of God. Joseph and his family did not. Dreams were one of the chief ways God spoke to those who did not yet have a Bible.

Pharaoh was so troubled that he sent for his magicians and wise men to ... (vs. 8) Choose one:

Cheer him up   Interpret his dreams   Commission his army

The Nile River was revered by the Egyptians as a god because of the fertile land it produced caused by the annual flooding of its banks. An ancient Egyptian text found by archaeologists contained praises to the Nile like one would make to a god because it was recognized as the cornerstone of Egypt's economy.[1] Pharaoh saw the Nile in his dreams, cattle and grain (both vital commodities to a thriving economy) consuming themselves, and knew that the financial forecast of his kingdom was in dire straits.

And here is where we see the miraculous truth that God had been continually working in Joseph's life to bring him to this very day. Pharaoh desperately needed to know what was the meaning of the dreams. The difficulty was that his magicians and wise men proved themselves to be incapable to help him. The thought of the Nile River, cattle, and grain being involved in an economic crisis may not have been able to be comprehended by these men who had no reference point to these staples of the Egyptian economy being

threatened. The "wise" men quickly realized that none of their magic was going to bring Pharaoh the answer he was so earnestly seeking. Just when all hope seemed gone, the king's cupbearer remembered whom he had forgotten two years before – a certain Hebrew slave had correctly interpreted his own dream which restored the cupbearer to his present position.

After reading Genesis 41:9-13, what words of the cupbearer do you think persuaded Pharaoh to act?

Write out Genesis 41:14 here and underline the word that describes how Pharaoh sent for Joseph:

Can you even imagine, my dear sister, what must have been going through Joseph's mind as he left the prison he had called home over the last two years for the grandest residence in all of Egypt? Was he calm as he shaved and changed his clothes? Was he remembering his beloved father as he walked the long corridor into the throne room of Pharaoh? Did the faces of the ten brothers that had sent him to Egypt smite him again with fresh agony? A sharing of his dreams had been part of the reason why he had been thrown into the first prison - the empty well - by his brothers. Now he was being called on to interpret another dream. Did his soul stir within him that God was very present with Joseph as his feet walked him into Pharaoh's presence.

You and I do not need to try to manipulate those in authority over us.

Look carefully at Genesis 41:15-16. Who does Joseph give credit to for the interpretation of the dreams of Pharaoh?

Pharaoh was considered a god to the Egyptians. We cannot underestimate the absolute courage Joseph had to answer Pharaoh the way he did. Joseph told Pharaoh that Jehovah alone deserved the glory for revealing the dreams to Joseph.

After reading Genesis 41:17-32, pay careful attention to Joseph's words in verse 31. Joseph's own life experience paralleled Pharaoh's dreams. He had experienced years of abundance as the darling of his father, only to have years of famine as a slave and then as a prisoner, which made his former life as the favorite son of his father in Canaan seem like a dream to him. He understood, perhaps better than anyone in that throne room, the absolute validity of Pharaoh's dreams.

How much do we trust God, my dear sister? I am deeply challenged in my own impulsiveness or desire to manipulate a situation when I look at Joseph's restraint before Pharaoh in the next four verses of the chapter. Joseph did not say, *Hey, Pharaoh, I am the man for the job!* Instead, he calmly laid out the facts to Pharaoh and put his life in the hands of Jehovah.

Where does Proverbs 21:1 tell us the heart of the king is and who directs it?

You and I do not need to try to manipulate those in authority over us. We don't need to boast to our boss about why we deserve the position we want. Our God has power over those who could promote us or our husbands. He is also in charge of the timing of our promotions. That does not mean that we do not work hard as unto the Lord, but our job is to be still and know that He is God.

Look at Genesis 41:37-45 and list all that Pharaoh did for Joseph:

My dear sister, what have you and I convinced ourselves is impossible, even though we belong to the Creator of the universe? Have we forgotten that our God is on His throne today, aware of not only of our needs, but also our heart's greatest longing? In one day, Joseph the slave became the prince of Egypt. In one day, the one who had no rights was set completely free and given a position of great honor. In one day, the forgotten one became second only to the king himself. And that, my dear friend, is how our God works. The One who numbers the very hairs on our heads is capable of moving mountains for us. I can think of no better way to end this lesson than with the following words inspired by the Holy Spirit. May they encourage us in a fresh way if we are struggling with weariness in being faithful in our obedience to Christ:

Have we forgotten that our God is on His throne today, aware of not only of our needs, but also our heart's greatest longing?

Let us not become weary in doing good, for at the proper time we will reap a harvest if we do not give up. ***Galatians 6:9***

Jesus looked at them and said, "With man this is impossible, but with God all things are possible." ***Matthew 19:26***

Humble yourselves, therefore, under God's mighty hand, that he may lift you up in due time. Cast all your anxiety on him because he cares for you.
1 Peter 5:6-7

Day Two – The Great Exchange

I can scarcely imagine what Joseph must have thought as he was ushered out of the throne room of Pharaoh. He had entered a forgotten Hebrew slave. He left as the Hebrew prime minister of all of Egypt! How often has history ever told the story of a ruler who rewards the second highest position in his kingdom to a foreigner? But when the King of the universe holds the heart of the earthly king in His hands, the improbable becomes reality.

Let's refresh our memories about yesterday's lesson. Please read Genesis 41:41-57 and continue to see how drastically Joseph's life changed after interpreting Pharaoh's dreams:

Compare Genesis 37:2 with Genesis 41:46. How long had Joseph been a slave in Egypt when he was promoted by Pharaoh? Circle one:

Five years   Eleven years   Thirteen years   Twenty years

How long have you been waiting for a change in your life? Does Joseph's story give you hope that God is in control of the clock? Share here:

There are some life-transforming lessons we miss because we simply get tired of waiting for God to act.

We have the advantage of seeing the journey of Joseph through the eyes of a complete story. Our life story, however, is still being written. I have a friend whom I have prayed with once a week for the last four years. Together, she and I have pleaded with God for one main request during the hundreds of times we have approached the throne of God. Our times of prayer could be evaluated as wasted time if an outside person peering in looked for the original change we have been begging God for during these many months of prayer. There has been undeniable change that has occurred, but not where my friend and I were initially hoping the change would happen. The most profound changes have happened in us individually as God has revealed how He wants us both to respond to the delayed answer to our initial request of Him. I know, beyond a shadow of a doubt, that we are praying within His will. There are some life-transforming lessons we miss because we simply get tired of waiting for God to act.

What do the following Scripture say about the benefits of perseverance?

Hebrews 10:35-36:

James 1:2-4:

James 1:12:

How do you see the above promises from Scripture were realized in Joseph's life?

Do you believe that God will do the same for you or have you thrown away your confidence in the wait?

How plentiful were the first seven years of abundance according to Genesis 41:49?

Our God is not bound by time.

Many years earlier, Joseph's great-grandfather, Abraham had received an unalterable and holy covenant from God Himself. In Genesis 22:17, God promised that He would make Abraham's descendants as numerous as the sand on the seashore. The daunting obstacle to the promise's fulfillment was that the son that God had promised to Abraham had not yet been born. Abraham died knowing his grandsons, Jacob and Esau, but he had been dead long before Joseph was born. Yet God continued to be faithful to the promise He had made years earlier.

How was God fulfilling His word to Abraham Genesis 22:18 through Joseph's new duties?

What does 2 Peter 3:9 tell us about God's timetable?

We are such earth-bound creatures. We live in a world that demands instant gratification. Our God is not bound by time. He does not keep a schedule. That fact is distressing when I am impatiently waiting for something, but how glad I am that He is patient with me! Some changes in me have taken years and have been so small that I sometimes wonder if there would be a noticeable change if I had a thousand years to work on that frustrating ungodly habit or attitude that needs to go. In those situations, I am so thankful that He is patient.

The abundance of the seven years before the famine manifested itself in Joseph's personal life. He became a married man and a father.

Write the meanings of the Hebrew names Joseph gave to his two sons (vv. 51-52):

Joseph had not forgotten what had happened to him over the last thirteen years of his life. I do believe that God had done a major work in Joseph's broken heart so that Manasseh's name was Joseph's expression of gratefulness to God that he could enjoy life again. I have a family member who lost her infant son to SIDS. In the smothering cloak of her fresh grief, she would feel guilty over laughing or feeling joy of any kind because her infant son was gone. Her grief overwhelmed her every thought in the months following her son's death. While there continue to be days when her grief is the dominant emotion she experiences, those days are less frequent than before. She can laugh again. She will never forget her son or ever stop missing him, but she has discovered that life does continue to have joy.

After reading Isaiah 61:1-3, fill in the following blanks that Jesus Christ longs to give us in exchange for our pain (verse 3):

Instead of ashes, a __________________ of beauty.
Instead of mourning, the __________ of ________________________.
Instead of a spirit of despair, a __________________ of praise.
They will be called oaks of righteousness, a planting of the Lord, for the display of his splendor.

May we have been taught well by our suffering not to repeat what has been done to us to others – even to the ones who were the perpetrators of our own grief.

Are you willing to see the Lord make these exchanges in your pain? Why?

I don't believe that Joseph could have had an Ephraim if he had not allowed God to start to heal his broken heart over all that had happened to him. Ladies, are we stuck in this place of obsessive remembrance of what has been done to us? Is the first thought that crosses our minds remembering the betrayal or the pain that we have experienced? Are we experiencing joy on a regular basis? When was the last time we felt unburdened enough to laugh with our whole hearts? If Joseph had been obsessed with revenge against his brothers, he could not have been an effective servant of Pharaoh during the years of abundance. He may have missed the opportunity for his own freedom had his mind been consumed with his pain. Do we remember what has happened to us? Yes, but only so the memory can serve us to understand that we also are capable of great sin against others also. May we have been taught well by our suffering not to repeat what has been done to us to others – even to the ones who were the perpetrators of our own grief.

What does Isaiah 43:18-19 tell us that God wants to do in our lives now?

It's time for these crushed bones of ours to rejoice. It is time for our thoughts to be on what is pure, lovely, and honorable. It is time for true joy to replace the pit of depression in which we may have found ourselves for too long. God the Father raised Jesus Christ from the dead! Surely He has the power to bring our crushed hearts back to life again!

But God will never demand the great exchange to happen in our lives. What does John 10:10 explain that we might not have known?

As we close, I would like us to make Psalm 139:23-24 our prayer. Use the space below to record what the Holy Spirit reveals is the obstacle to you walking in the abundant life Jesus has promised to you. I am praying for Him to speak to each one of us who is willing to search our hearts before Him.

It's time for these crushed bones of ours to rejoice.

Satan wants nothing more than to continue to rob us of what is rightfully ours – a joyful, abundant life in Christ. We are not doomed to just survive this life until heaven. We have been given all we need through the blood of Jesus Christ to *thrive* in this life! If our lives are a barren wasteland to the devastation that has happened to us, the glad news and incredible hope we have is that Jesus can take those barren places in our lives and give us abundance where Satan has stolen, killed, and destroyed. The choice is ours.

Joseph had faced many tests and passed them. God had exalted him to the highest seat of power under Pharaoh of Egypt, the most powerful ruler of the known world. The famine Joseph had predicted through God's revelation to Pharaoh was not only in Egypt, but throughout the whole world. Unbeknownst to Joseph, his biggest test lay just around the corner as a band of broken brothers were about to make their appearance. All that Joseph had learned through his suffering was going to be tested to the utmost.

Day Three – Where the Heart Runs Free

"But, Mom, it's just not fair! All of my friends at school are getting to do that!"

My daughter has just entered the teen years. I am starting to see the beginnings of a lifelong inner struggle that she has revealed in these words of protest which I am starting to hear from her lips more frequently. I think I vaguely remember similar words coming from my own lips in response to my mother.

One of the biggest lies you and I might be tempted to believe is that those of us who are obedient to Christ and His Lordship over our lives are living a life of deprivation. We can become envious when we compare the obedience that a surrendered life demands to those who are free to live life however they want. We are commanded by God to love, forgive, and act in a way that is impossible without the empowering of the Holy Spirit because our flesh cannot do what is required to please God. Those who do not submit to Christ seem to be free to behave, say, and do whatever suits them, with little or no consequences. And, frankly, their lifestyles can come with consequences that affect our lives, too.

Those who do not submit to Christ seem to be free to behave, say, and do whatever suits them, with little or no consequences.

What had Asaph falsely come to believe in Psalm 73:13-14? Has this been your struggle? Share here:

Life can become difficult when we do not realize how utterly miserable and without peace are those who are not obeying Christ in their lives. I love Scripture because it tells the truth. Scripture exposes motives. Although we humans can work very hard to cover up what is really going on, the Word of God leaves no room for pretenses.

Although Joseph had allowed God to heal his broken heart over being so mistreated by his brothers, he may have been tempted to believe that the ten siblings were enjoying life back in Canaan. After all, they had never been slaves or prisoners. They had been free men or had they? Our story is going to dramatically change today as two worlds that have been separated for almost twenty years meet in a head-on collision.

After reading Genesis 42:1-6, answer the following questions:

What do you imagine was Jacob's tone in verses 1-2? Circle your answer:

Exasperated Loving Gentle

Write down the words used to identify Jacob's offspring in verses 3-6:

Verse 3: Verse 4:

Verse 5: Verse 6:

Joseph had been presumed dead by his father for almost twenty years. Yet, his name is mentioned to identify this group of brothers, even the favored Benjamin, in three out of the four verses above. I see a father who still had unhealthy control over sons that were fully grown. I see ten sons' independence hindered by their desperate need for assurance by their father that he loved them, too.

What were the motives of the brothers behind the wicked plot to get rid of Joseph according to Genesis 37:4, 11?

What insight does Romans 3:14-17 give us on the lives of the brothers because of what they had done to Joseph?

Although Joseph was in prison, who was with him in Genesis 39:20-21?

Joseph's prison may have been a physical one, but what made his situation bearable was that the Lord was with Joseph in that prison cell! The ten brothers never knew a life of peace during the twenty years they had covered up the horrible sin they had committed against their brother. Their prison, though invisible, was the most fortified and torturous. Sin's prison door offers no key of release. May we never be deceived into thinking that obeying Christ is anything other than true freedom, no matter how "free" others appear in their sinful lifestyle!

After reading Genesis 42:7-20, record your observations on the following:

- Why do you think Joseph immediately recognized his brothers although they did not recognize him? There are no wrong answers as this is from your perspective.

Verse nine tells us that Joseph remembered his dreams about them. How many stars bowed down in Genesis 37:9? How many brothers made the trip to Egypt?

What clue in Genesis 42:19 might we uncover as to Joseph's motive for not revealing his identity at this time?

Dr. Andrew Schmutzer, a professor at Moody Bible Institute, has provided a thought-provoking series of lectures on the life of Joseph. Human relationships are complex. Many theologians have offered the story of Joseph as a simple tale of estranged brothers who are forgiven by the one who was betrayed. Before life experience forced me to look more deeply into the ugly face of bitterness caused by betrayal and the work that I continue to have to allow the Holy Spirit to perform in me, I would have judged Joseph's actions of throwing the brothers in prison here as an act of revenge. I do not believe that this is true anymore.

The book of Proverbs was written so that its readers would gain wisdom as well as, "for giving prudence to the simple, knowledge and discretion to the young" (Proverbs 1:1). We especially need wisdom in relationships where there has been loss of trust.

We especially need wisdom in relationships where there has been loss of trust.

Match the following passages of Scripture with their correct reference:

The righteous are cautious in friendship.	Proverbs 2:11
A fool gives full vent to his anger, but a wise man keeps himself under control.	Proverbs 10:19
When words are many, sin is not absent, but he who holds his tongue is wise.	Proverbs 12:26
Discretion will protect you, and understanding will guard you.	Proverbs 29:11

We have to remember that the home which reared Joseph and the ten brothers was built on envy among four women. Jacob's blatant favoritism of Joseph was the obstacle to any genuine emotion of love or care coming from the ten sons of Leah, Bilhah, and Zilpah toward the son of Rachel. How many times have we heard of the heartache that follows an emotional reunion between lost or separated family members? Scripture indicates that Joseph never had a close relationship with his ten older siblings.

Let's remind ourselves of the status of the relationship between Joseph and his brothers in Genesis 37:4: "...they __________ him and could not speak a kind ________ to him."

What did the brothers confess to Joseph, who remained unrecognized by them under harsh interrogation in Genesis 42:13?

Does that strike you as odd? Unconfessed sin and toxic secrets have a way of slipping out at the oddest times. The brothers had carried around their guilt for over twenty years and had not divulged their secret to their father. Yet here, in front of someone they believed to be a stranger, their mouths revealed the guilt which they still carried in their hearts.

What does Numbers 32:23 tell us will eventually happen when there is unconfessed sin in our lives?

Unconfessed sin and toxic secrets have a way of slipping out at the oddest times.

What was revealed by the brothers that made Joseph weep in Genesis 42:21-24? How do you think this information might have made Joseph feel about Reuben?

Let's now read Genesis 42:25-38. What frightening discovery did one of the brothers make when they stopped to feed their donkeys on the return trip to Canaan (v. 28)?

One of my siblings had feet that turned in toward themselves which warranted the need for corrective shoes fastened to twister cables. I remember having to go to a hospital for crippled children to have his braces adjusted every three months. I wanted to scream to the people who passed us in the hall with looks of pity on their faces that my little brother was not crippled. I hated that place. I hated its smell and the dimly lit hallway where I had to sit while my brother's feet were examined. But I detested even more the knowledge that I had no choice but to return again three months later.

I cannot imagine how it was finally decided among the ten who was going to tell Daddy Jacob what the lord of all Egypt demanded as a condition for their imprisoned brother to be released and for their households not to starve. The house of Jacob was between a rock and a hard place. The brothers had no choice but to return to Egypt.

How did Jacob react to this news in Genesis 42:36?

Write out the reason for Jacob's refusal to let Benjamin return with his brothers to Egypt in verse 38?

Although Joseph's presence had been missing for over twenty years, Jacob kept him alive through his blatant favoritism toward the sons of his beloved Rachel. He had never embraced the ten sons who had been born to him first and with whom he still had living at home. No, my dear sisters, Joseph had not been missing out on a joyful life in Canaan, but had been spared years from a home filled with anger, bitterness, jealousy, and toxic secrets. Solomon was right when he wrote:

All the days of the oppressed are wretched, but the cheerful heart has a continual feast (Proverbs 15:15).

The cost of obedience that is required to walk in paths of freedom pales in comparison to the alternative of living with the burden of guilt and shame that accompanies sin.

God was with Joseph in prison, using the injustice committed against Joseph to transform him into a wise and discerning man. Sadly, the ten brothers who put him there had no such experience.

You and I should not envy those who live with the burden of guilt caused by their refusal to bow in submission to Jesus Christ. The cost of obedience that is required to walk in paths of freedom pales in comparison to the alternative of living with the burden of guilt and shame that accompanies sin. We are not deprived when we obey. We are rich! What we may not have comprehended is that God, in His infinite mercy, has possibly rescued us from a path of destruction and misery we would have surely taken had we decided not to obey Him. May we have eyes to see the truth: obedience to His commands allows us to run free, even if the other party does not join in the redeeming work Christ offers in relationships. We escape the stranglehold of guilt with our obedience to forgive. Praise Him with me, my precious sister, that obedience to our Jesus allows us to be truly free!

I run in the path of your commands, for you have set my heart free.
Psalm 119:45

Day Four – Famine's Table

There are some experiences I witnessed as a child growing up in a third world country that are forever branded on my brain. A memory that has stayed with me for thirty years was the day a man came to our mission station during our lunch hour begging my mother to do something for his baby. Although the child was around one year of age, he weighed between six and eight pounds. The sharp angles of the bones lying just beneath the pinched, malnourished skin of his face contrasted with his huge, vacant eyes. There was nothing my mother could do for that precious little soul who left this earth about an hour later. His small body had finally succumbed to the ravaging effects caused by lack of food.

Fill in the blanks from Lamentations 4:9: "Those killed by the ________________ are better off than those who die from ______________________; racked with hunger they waste away for lack of ___________ from the field."

A starving stomach is a fact that is hard to ignore. Starvation is a slow and painful process, resulting in a truly horrible death. Our lesson ended yesterday with Jacob adamantly declaring that Benjamin would never go back to Egypt with his other sons. But watching the bins of grain diminish over time produced a desperation that forced a change of heart.

Grief not observed in a healthy manner has the potential to destroy a person.

I have never known the pain of physical hunger, but I have known desperation. How has God used desperation to bring you to a decision you did not want to make?

Let's pick up our study by reading Genesis 43 in its entirety.

Grief not observed in a healthy manner has the potential to destroy a person. Mix grief with selfishness and a refusal to heal and the results may be catastrophic to many. Jacob had known about the condition for buying more grain in Egypt since his sons had returned months ago, yet he stubbornly clung to his own will rather than doing what was best for his family. It seems that this had been a pattern all of his life. Instead of acting lovingly toward Leah, he had continually shown favoritism toward Rachel and her sons. The jealousy and hatred of the ten older sons toward Rachel and Joseph, and Jacob's unwillingness to ask God to help him love all of his children, made reconciliation impossible. When Joseph was gone, instead of crying out to God to heal his family, Jacob's favoritism then shifted to Joseph's younger brother, Benjamin.

What did Jacob ask his sons in verse 6?

Jacob blamed his sons for his own problem with relinquishing control. The trouble was not that they were not willing to return to help feed their father and their households. The trouble was that Jacob, in his selfishness, refused to agree to the conditions which would save the entire family. How does it make us feel when we are blamed for someone else's selfishness or unwillingness to change? Jacob, instead of being grateful that God had provided a way for his family to be rescued from a slow, painful death caused by the famine, shamed his sons for conditions over which they had no control.

After reading Psalm 69:19-20, answer the following questions:

What three words does the psalmist use to describe himself in verse 19?

________________ ________________ ________________

What is the tragic result of these descriptions in verse 20?

Hurt people hurt people.

I am not excusing the brothers' heinous act toward Joseph in any way, but as we look at those we need to forgive (including ourselves), could our recognition of the role of rejection and shame in their lives shed light on the cause of brokenness in the one who has hurt us? Hurt people hurt people. Rejection and shame destroy and break hearts. People with unhealed broken hearts desperately look for comforters, but nothing this world can offer them will bind up and heal their brokenness, so they remain heartbroken, often breaking others' hearts as a result.

Where do the faces of scorn, shame, and /or disgrace show themselves in your own struggle to forgive?

What can only Jesus Christ do for us according to Psalm 147:3?

Joseph was not the only person in the family whose life had been radically changed. We have seen glimpses into the hearts of the ones who sold Joseph as a slave. The brothers had unknowingly confessed the gnawing collective guilt they had lived with over their actions toward Joseph. Tragic events happening in the lives of the three oldest sons of Leah (Reuben, Simon and Levi) before Joseph's slavery had affected both their lives and standings within the family (see Genesis 49:3-7). The fourth born son of Leah now stepped up and stood up to Jacob.

Briefly state what each of the following references tells us about Judah:

Genesis 37:26-27:

Genesis 38:25-26:

Use three words to describe Judah's character based on the above two Scriptures:

Use three words to describe Judah's character in Genesis 43:8-10:

We do not know what God may be doing in the life of the one who has hurt us to bring about change! We see our pain only from our perspective. We have no window into the other person's hurt. Our God knows the beginning from the end. In His infinite omniscience, He knows best how to handle the person who has hurt us. We may want revenge. We fuss and fume and become bitter because He chooses to be merciful to the one who has caused us such pain. Why doesn't He just give her/him what we think is deserved? Because He is the Redeemer. He is slow to anger and abounding in love. He is not willing that any should perish. We must let Him be Lord over our hurt and Lord over the one who has caused it.

We must let Him be Lord over our hurt and Lord over the one who has caused it.

What sobering reminder does James 2:12-13 give us?

Have I betrayed someone? Yes. Have I taken what wasn't mine? Yes. Have I been spiteful and vindictive? Yes. I, too, have broken someone's trust who should have been able to depend on me. I am a lawbreaker, too. Do I want mercy? Without question! How can I begrudge God's mercy toward another when He has lavished mercy on me?

What did Judah's courage do in Jacob in Genesis 43:11-15?

And so a fragile band of brothers hurried back to Egypt and presented themselves before the one who had demanded that they return with Benjamin. Judah had stepped up as the new leader of the family. The brothers had met the conditions placed on them to buy more grain after finally convincing their father of the necessity of bringing his favorite son with them.

What shocking location were the brothers taken to when they arrived? Circle one:

The dungeon The executioner's block Joseph's house

List the four wrongs they believed Joseph would do to them in verse 18:

To the pure, all things are pure, but to those who are corrupted and do not believe, nothing is pure. In fact, both their minds and consciences are corrupted.

– Titus 1:15

Do we ever sit in confusion over why our kindness is misunderstood? We want to forgive. We want reconciliation, but it seems impossible because our actions are continually misconstrued by the other person. To a guilty conscience, every action is scrutinized with suspicion. There is no price that can be put on being at peace with God and man which comes from having a clear conscience. The brothers were terrified because they were afraid that Joseph was going to attack them, overpower them, and make them slaves – the very sins they committed against him over twenty years earlier.

Their fear, unbridled by God's Spirit, was not rational or restrained.

There is no price that can be put on being at peace with God and man which comes from having a clear conscience.

What does Philippians 4:6-7 tell us to do when we are anxious? Do you see the brothers doing this?

Go back to list above of the wrongs the brothers believed Joseph was going to commit against them in Genesis 43:18 and, next to each imagined wrong, list what Joseph did for them through his steward in verses 23-24.

Those are not the actions of a bitter, vindictive person. Those are the actions of a wounded heart that decides to let mercy triumph over judgment! The brothers had been wrong. They had misjudged this man that had spoken harshly to them for reasons they did not have enough information about to fairly process. Joseph's disguise was not vindictive, but was the only way to test if the brothers had matured in the face of the favoritism that had made them act maliciously against him so long ago. The ten had once left Joseph for dead because of their jealousy over their father's love. They had now returned to Egypt to reclaim their imprisoned brother Simeon and save their families from starvation. They had fulfilled Joseph's nearly impossible condition of coming back with the one whose existence had given them a lesser place in their father's affections. Joseph was not the only one who had been affected by what God had allowed in this broken family.

What did the brothers not realize their actions in verses 26 and 28 were fulfilling in Genesis 37:9?

What knowledge in Genesis 43:28 and 29-30 caused Joseph to weep?

When was the last time you cried over receiving good news?

What astonished the brothers in verse 33?

Although the brothers felt relaxed enough to eat and drink freely at the table, the biggest shock of their lives lay just around the corner. A famine in Canaan had forced Jacob's family to have to begin to confront the famine in their souls. I wonder if the Lord is slowly revealing to us how He has been working all along in the famine of our relationships. It's just like Him to prepare a banquet for us when a feast is what we are least expecting. He cannot be figured out, no matter how hard we may try. Let's praise Him that He knows what He is doing – even in the barren places of our lives. He is at work!

Day Five – A Costly Confession

As I am writing this lesson, my children have a half day of school left before they experience ten weeks of summer freedom from school work. They are beside themselves with excitement as they anticipate a break from the routine of a schedule dictated by homework and extra-curricular activities. I smile in remembrance of my own excitement over school days ending for another year – except over the memories of one summer. That was the summer of 1989 when I was twenty-one years old.

My father was recovering from a closed-head injury he received as a result of a nearly fatal accident in Congo that June. I had been living a double life in front of my parents. Always eager to please, I decided that I should hide the truth from them that I was in involved in a relationship with a young man of which they did not approve. The secrecy was exactly what Satan delighted in as he tormented me with the thought that God was punishing me for my sinful behavior through my father's accident. I was wracked with guilt. I would run into my room and stifle my sobs in my pillow as I would see my father struggle to heal from his brain injury. But I just couldn't tell anyone! What would everyone think of me? The summer of 1989 was anything but enjoyable as I wallowed alone in my guilt.

We have seen the ravages of guilt in the dysfunctional family of Jacob. Getting rid of Joseph did not solve the brothers' deep wounding caused by Jacob's overt favoritism toward Joseph. The brothers had come to the heartbreaking conclusion that their sin against Joseph had brought the crippling emotion of guilt to compound their pain. Satan goads us on in our hatred and then accuses us with relentless guilt after we have committed treacherous acts against others. He is a heartless condemner.

Satan goads us on in our hatred and then accuses us with relentless guilt after we have committed treacherous acts against others.

Let's look up the following passages and record what unconfessed guilt does to our souls:

Psalm 38:1-4:

Psalm 51:3:

Psalm 109:6-7:

Ezra 9:5-7:

Guilt was a merciless whip that had beaten the ten brothers for over twenty years. Can you imagine the heaviness of carrying around the secret of what they had done to Joseph? A twisted transformation takes place in our souls when we are afraid of being found out. Life becomes an exhausting and fearful exercise of deceit as we try to keep hidden what we have done. We falsely believe that the truth will condemn us, when exactly the opposite is true.

Let's continue our story today by reading Genesis 44:1-13.

What item did Joseph instruct his steward to place in all the brothers' sacks? Circle one:

Egyptian pottery   Their returned silver

A letter from Pharaoh

What was this item used for in Genesis 37:28?

The silver had reappeared not once, not twice, but three times. What do you think that did to their guilty consciences? I remember reading a story of a young man convicted of manslaughter whose sentence was to write the victim's family a check for one dollar on a given day every year. The reminder was almost more than the young man could bear.

What relief does 1 John 1:9 give us about our confessed sin?

If we have been carrying around the burden of our unconfessed sin, guilt is eating us alive! Our God is faithful and just to forgive and then cleanse us from that guilt through the shed blood of His Son, Jesus Christ. Some of us, however, are letting Satan convince us that Christ is not powerful enough to do what Scripture clearly declares in 1 John 1:9. How tragic that we have been shackled needlessly because we choose not to believe that Jesus has forgiven us and made us clean.

Our God is faithful and just to forgive and then cleanse us from that guilt through the shed blood of His Son, Jesus Christ.

What had Joseph instructed his steward to put in Benjamin's sack (Gen. 44:2)?

What rash promise did the brothers make when the steward accused them of stealing the cup in Genesis 44:9?

How did the steward change the brothers' proposed penalty in verse 10?

What did the brothers do in response to what was found in Benjamin's sack (vs. 13)? Circle one:

Attacked the steward   Tore their clothes

Accused each other

We do not have a point of reference in the western world to adequately understand the level of grief that the tearing of their garments signified in the brothers. They were completely beside themselves with terror and despondency at the revelation of the cup's whereabouts. The ones who had turned deaf ears toward the cries of the favored brother they heartlessly sold into slavery now were in utter despair at the thought of Benjamin, the sole replacement in their father's affections, being doomed to the same fate. The charade had gone on too long.

After reading Genesis 44:14-17, how did the brothers respond to seeing Joseph?

Never in his wildest imaginations would the seventeen-year-old Joseph have pictured the fulfillment of his dreams in Genesis 37:7-9 happening this way. There could not have been any pleasure in Joseph watching his brothers practically scrape their noses as they groveled before him. There had been too much pain, too many dashed dreams and unmet expectations to allow Joseph to revel in this moment. The collective anguish of all twelve in the room must have been almost unbearable.

Let's continue reading Genesis 44:15-34.

Which brother came forward to beg for Benjamin's life? Circle one:

Reuben　　Simeon　　Judah　　Benjamin

Judah's plea for Benjamin is one of the most heart-wrenching speeches in all of Scripture. The rawness of his words makes me weep as the deepest wounds of his heart are exposed. It chronicles the transformation of an entitled, self-absorbed man to one who was willing to lose his own freedom to spare his baby brother from a life of misery as well as the father who had never given him the love he had craved since he was a little boy. Judah's world had been destroyed as he watched the jealous competition between his unloved mother with her sister Rachel. This Judah was the same brother whose idea it was to sell Joseph to a living death. This same Judah had an incestuous relationship with his daughter-in-law who conceived because he had been deceived into thinking she was a prostitute. This was Judah now standing humbled and broken before the brother he had betrayed, but could not yet recognize.

What family skeletons did Judah bring out into the open in verse 20? How did Judah speak of Jacob in the last words of verse 20?

Can you empathize with Judah's painful admission that his father loved his brother, while knowing that he had been overlooked? If yes, please share here:

Jacob had four wives – two sisters that came through two marriage ceremonies and two that became his wives because of the intense jealousy between the sisters. How many wives did Jacob say he had in verse 27? How do you think this statement affected the ten older brothers of Benjamin standing before Joseph?

What desperate plea did Judah make to Joseph in vv. 33-34?

Dr. Andrew Schmutzer said this about the necessity of confession:

"Where there is catastrophe in families, [and] where there has been no meaningful admission of guilt, healing and reconciliation are impossible ... Reconciliation does not come that easily when trust and respect have been broken." [3]

How important is confession of guilt? Let's read the words of the psalmist in Psalm 32 together and answer the following questions:

What did the psalmist experience before his confession in vv. 3-4?

What happened to change his anguish in verse 5?

What did he find to be true after his confession in verse 6?

How has respect and trust been trampled on when you consider your own struggle with forgiveness? How has this affected the possibility of reconciliation?

"Where there is catastrophe in families, [and] where there has been no meaningful admission of guilt, healing and reconciliation are impossible ..."
– Dr. Andrew Schmutzer

"The Lord is my Strength, my personal bravery, and my invincible army; He makes my feet like hinds feet and will make me to walk (not to stand still in terror, but to walk) and make (spiritual) progress upon my high places (of trouble, suffering or responsibility)!"

– Habakkuk 3:19 (AMP)

Joseph had been summoned to the high place of suffering, trouble, and responsibility. We are about to see what the dark night of the soul had produced in Joseph. High places are treacherous because they can be the death of us if we walk on them without the empowering of God Himself. If we have not surrendered our flesh as we try to navigate our places of suffering, trouble, and responsibility, the fall we take can be devastating to us and all we touch. Can God trust us to to be as faithful as Joseph was during our times of supreme testing?

Until now, Joseph could not fully trust the brothers with his identity. The ever-appearing silver was not a warped mind game Joseph was playing, but was used in a series of tests on the brothers to see if changes had happened in them which would help to sustain a future relationship. The final and crucial test Joseph had placed on the brothers had finally been passed with Judah's plea. Joseph knew that the brothers would not betray and abandon Benjamin as they had Joseph to the Ishmaelite slave traders. He had heard of the intense anguish that his departure had made on the family. His father, Jacob, was still alive but time was running short. We are about to see one of the most jaw-dropping revelations ever recorded in human history.

The Plan of Glory

There was a man who asked God to show him His glory. God promised Moses that He would do what Moses had asked. If I were Moses, I would have been beside myself anticipating God's answer to my request with visions of some miraculous wonder that God would cause to happen in front of my eyes. Perhaps He would put on a fireworks display of stars in the heavens. Maybe He would allow me to gaze upon heaven for a dazzling moment. Surely His glory would proclaim undeniably who He was in some thunderous, earth-shattering, unforgettable way.

In response to Moses' request, God told Moses that He was going to hide him in the cleft of a rock, put His hand over him, and declare the following words as He passed by Moses:

"... I will cause all my goodness to pass in front of you, and I will proclaim my name, the LORD, in your presence. I will have mercy on whom I will have mercy, and I will have compassion on whom I will have compassion. But," he said, "you cannot see my face, for no one may see me and live."

Exodus 33:19-20

No face-to-face encounter? Being hidden away in a rock? And a declaration of mercy and compassion on whom God chooses? *That is God's glory?*

And my human reaction would have been:

"No, God, I want the fireworks display! That can't be what Your glory looks like!"

My precious friend, have we balked at God's plan of glory in our struggle to forgive? In fact, because His plan does not look at all like we were expecting, we may have missed it altogether. It is profound to me that Moses was hidden in the rock because the glory of God would have killed him had he been able to look fully, unprotected into that Glory. Part of God's glory is His right to decide who receives His mercy and compassion – even to those whom we would want to receive His vengeance.

This week will focus on the benefits of forgiveness which extend far beyond our costly obedience. We will learn the glorious purpose of God in Joseph's life as we stand in awe of the plan of glory revealed. A plan that did not look anything like Joseph may have expected as a seventeen-year-old boy granted God-given dreams.

We will leave this week with a gnawing question: Did reconciliation between Joseph and his brothers ever take place? May the only wise God come to our aid and comfort as we grapple with that question in our own difficult relationships.

Day One – A Stunning Reunion

If you were to accompany me to the video store, my choice for a great movie would be found in the drama section. I don't like drama in my own life, but I love to watch a complex story unfold before my eyes. A great story line to me would be one that explored the depths of human emotions and made me laugh with joy and weep in empathy in the process. The best stories are ones that are interwoven with complicated characters placed in situations that are relatable to me. The story of the family that we have studied these last six weeks has contained all of those elements. The difference is that our great God has been the author of this family epic. Through His Holy Spirit, I pray that we have seen our own story within the chapters of Genesis.

How has God specifically spoken to you through the study of Joseph's life?

Today's reading is so rich in its complexity. We need to ask the Holy Spirit to reveal Himself through the verses of Genesis 45. Joseph had recognized his brothers from the moment he laid eyes on them, but he remained a stranger to them. After Joseph presented several tests to see if his brothers were changed men, his emotions were at their pinnacle as he wrestled with revealing his true identity to the ten brothers who had robbed him of the identity he had once had before slavery in Egypt.

Let's read Genesis 45:1-5 and ponder all that takes place in these verses together.

What did Joseph order to happen in verse 1? Circle one:

Prison for Judah   Egyptian servants to leave

Benjamin taken away

What did the Egyptians hear and why in verse 2?

My parents are currently in Congo where they spend half the year at the mission station where I grew up. My mother told me that one of the staff members just lost his third child in a span of eighteen months. The last two children died of malaria within six months of each other. A Congolese funeral is very different than our American funerals. The entire village comes together to mourn with the family over the deceased. Instead of the quiet tears or sobs of the family members at the end of a receiving line like we are used to in the United States, the Congolese cry until they are hoarse. They wail and moan from the core of their beings. It may seem strange to us, but I believe the Congolese grieve in a much healthier way than we grieve here in America as we try to minimize our tears over what has happened to us.

Joseph's tears were like the bursting of a dam that had suddenly been breached. He, too, had experienced the death of all he had once known in his father's house. Now the very brothers who had stolen that life from him were groveling before him. He could not bear the secret of his identity anymore.

I am begging our God to be able to grip our hearts with the scene we have just read in the pages of our Bibles. There are some of us who have not wept like Joseph did over our pain and we desperately need to! Weeping does not undo the hurt we have experienced, but it acknowledges that the wounding happened instead of denying that the wound exists. When we stuff our hurt and refuse to go to the only One who can heal us, we walk around in a state of denial and become dead inside. We become jaded and suspicious and, most deadly of all, we may become bitter.

Listen to the following powerful quote about this danger:

There are some of us who have not wept like Joseph did over our pain and we desperately need to!

To love at all is to be vulnerable. Love anything and your heart will be wrung and possibly broken. If you want to make sure of keeping it intact you must give it to no one, not even an animal. Wrap it carefully round with hobbies and little luxuries; avoid all entanglements. Lock it up safe in the casket or coffin of your selfishness. But in that casket, safe, dark, motionless, airless, it will change. It will not be broken; it will become unbreakable, impenetrable, irredeemable. To love is to be vulnerable.[1]

– C.S. Lewis from The Four Loves

What does Matthew 7:6 command us not to do?

Listen to the words of the eighteenth-century theologian, John Wesley, on what this verse means:

That is, talk not of the deep things of God to those whom you know to be wallowing in sin. Neither declare the great things God hath done for your soul to the profane, furious, persecuting wretches. Talk not of perfection, for instance, to the former; not of your experience to the latter. But our Lord does in nowise forbid us to reprove, as occasion is, both the one and the other.[2]

Ladies, we must be wise women with our tears and with those to whom we would pour out our hearts. Joseph could not cry in front of his brothers until now. The tests he had put them through over the last many months had shown that they were changed and broken men, now worthy of his tears. Some people are not worthy of witnessing our deepest griefs. We must pour out our hearts to God in those situations all the while fighting to keep our hearts soft and not hardened towards Him.

What does verse 3 reveal to us about the emotional state of the brothers?

Terrified? Sometimes I think that the English language does not have an adequate word to describe an emotion. The brothers' heads were spinning because this man whom they still did not recognize had ordered everyone from the room. As soon as they were alone with him, they witnessed cries from the depths of Joseph's soul which were so loud that they could be heard by the Egyptians. And then, without the help of an interpreter, these shocking words came from Joseph's lips:

"I am Joseph!"

Describe what you believe the brothers felt when they heard Joseph's admission:

We need to start asking ourselves, *What riches have I found in my pain that I can praise God for? What has He rescued me from?*

It was *not* a relief! The words represented their worst nightmare come true. Why? Because Joseph had the power to treat them as they had treated him. The guilty see through blind eyes of suspicion. Those who do not give grace, do not expect grace in return. Seeing their stunned faces and frozen stances, Joseph had to ask his brothers to come close to him. No doubt, that distance was made up of the longest short distance of their lives.

What does Proverbs 4:7-8 tell us to purchase and at what cost. Why?

It is costly, my dear sister, to be wise! We do not learn what is most valuable except at great personal cost to our flesh and expectations. Joseph was not one of his brothers. He had been plucked from a dysfunctional family because God, in His infinite wisdom, had a plan for Joseph that He could not fulfill if Joseph's life had stayed as it had been at home with his father. As heartbreaking as some of our life experiences are, sometimes our awful circumstances are the catalyst to us learning truths that would have eluded us had we been allowed a life of no suffering. Has our pain caused us to realize the gaping need we have for Jesus Christ? Have we seen how disobedience in others is not the joy ride it may initially appear to be? We need to start asking ourselves, *What riches have I found in my pain that I can praise God for? What has He rescued me from?*

How did Joseph identify himself in verse 4?

What did he immediately tell them after this identification in verse 5?

The word *grace* means *unmerited favor.* In return for all of the distress that his brothers had caused him, Joseph refused to return the same treatment to them. Forgiveness is supernatural, my darling friend. It cannot be conjured up. It cannot be given freely without cost to the giver.

What is the reward for a godly response in the following Scriptures?

Psalm 22:24:

Proverbs 3:32:

Proverbs 25:21-22:

Matthew 5:44-48:

1 John 3:10:

What profound statement did Joseph make in Genesis 45:7-8?

Forgiveness is supernatural, my darling friend. It cannot be conjured up. It cannot be given freely without cost to the giver.

Joseph's willingness to forgive allowed him to be taken into the Lord's confidence. God had revealed to Joseph the redeeming work that He had accomplished, despite the sin of the brothers. Was Joseph wounded. Absolutely. But it was no longer just pain, but pain with purpose. Do you and I need to reframe our pain? What new level of healing would we experience if we understood that our God has been in control all along with a purpose greater than we could possibly imagine? Our identity need not be in our pain, but in our Redeemer!

Joseph was not vindictive. Our next passage proves this. After reading Genesis 45:9-15, list all that Joseph promised his brothers and his amazing act in vs. 15:

Let's close today's lesson by reading Genesis 45:16-24.

How did Pharaoh receive the news that Joseph's brothers had come in vv. 17-20?

Continue listing Joseph's generosity in verses 21-23.

What were Joseph's parting words to his brothers in verse 24?

Not even Joseph could have imagined how God would reward him for wrestling through the costly process of forgiveness.

Hilarious! Well, maybe not so hilarious come to think of it. I can imagine all of the possible finger-pointing and potential arguing over who was going to tell Jacob in a convincing manner that the son he had thought was dead all these years was ruler over all of Egypt! The stories of God's glory are anything but predictable! Not even Joseph could have imagined how God would reward him for wrestling through the costly process of forgiveness. But then again, when God writes the screenplay of our lives, the following promise can be ours, no matter what has happened! Let's cling to our faithful God who is bigger than our pain.

For when you did awesome things that we did not expect,
you came down, and the mountains trembled before you.
Since ancient times no one has heard,
no ear has perceived,
no eye has seen any God besides you,
who acts on behalf of those who wait for him.
Isaiah 64:3-4

Day Two – Full Circle Moments

So with new clothes on their backs and twenty donkeys loaded down with goods given to them by a brother they had long believed was dead, the band of eleven brothers headed back over the desert sands. The most difficult and dreaded conversation of their lives with their father. I cannot help but wonder how the ten older brothers of Joseph decided to process all that had happened to them since their father Jacob had first asked them to go to Egypt to buy grain for their starving families. The journey from Egypt to Bethel in Canaan was not just a hop, skip, and a jump away in distance. The length of their trip would have taken longer due to the overwhelming generosity of Joseph visible in the extravagant gifts he had sent with the brothers to serve as proof that he was alive and well as viceroy of all Egypt. There would have been no shortage of time to relive in their minds the years since Joseph's disappearance had changed their father's personality.

What did Jacob refuse after he had seen the coat in Genesis 37:35? Circle one:

All food for 7 days   To talk with Leah

Comfort from his children

Trust is the foundational element in relationships.

Have you ever known someone who made the same refusal due to profound grief? Describe how this affected him/her emotionally:

Let's read Genesis 45:25-28.

How did Jacob receive his sons' news about Joseph in verse 26?

Trust is the foundational element in relationships. Is it any wonder that Jacob, the deceiver, was stunned and could not initially believe his sons' story? Jacob's life was peppered with the evil of lies. Jacob had been both the deceiver (with his brother Esau, his father Isaac, and his father-in-law, Laban) and the victim of deceit (marriage to Leah, Joseph's slavery) in every important relationship in his life. Scripture is very clear, my dear sisters, about the law of the harvest in our lives.

Write out Galatians 6:7 after reading Galatians 6:7-8:

Family members who lie to each other cannot recognize the truth when it is sitting right in front of them. Those who have made deception a way of life cannot trust others easily. Without the overwhelming show of Joseph's generosity toward his father as evidence to back up the brothers' seemingly absurd claim, Jacob would have been unable to believe that Joseph was alive.

What does verse 27 say the effect of finally believing that Joseph was alive had on Jacob's spirit?

Some of my fondest childhood memories, before my family became missionaries in Congo, were spent with my mother's parents. My grandparents' lives were the picture of the American dream. Each of them had come from very poor southern families and had determined to make a new life for themselves in the thriving Motor City of Detroit, Michigan during the years of the Great Depression. Both of them worked hard all of their lives. Although neither of them finished school beyond the eighth grade, their thirst for knowledge never stopped.

My grandparents were sixty years old when I was born. I loved going to their house because I could always depend on the comfort of a routine. I only remember taking one trip with them to Frankenmuth, Michigan, a town that is decorated like Christmas all year round. Most of my memories at my grandparents' home center around playing outside as my grandmother hung out her laundry on the clothes line (she didn't want to waste electricity for the dryer!) or watching my grandfather tend his large garden where the best-tasting fruits and vegetables were grown. Grandma always pulled out the same white blanket and laid it on the carpet in front of the television after supper on Saturday evenings so that my sister and I could have a front row seat to *The Lawrence Welk Show*. We always had a big bowl of buttered popcorn and a homemade chocolate malt that Grandma had made in her blender. Nothing ever changed at my grandparents. I loved the security of the sameness of the routine during my visits with them.

Change is difficult at any age, but especially when someone is one hundred and thirty years old! Let's read Genesis 46:1-7.

Where did Israel (Jacob) first stop on his way to see Joseph and what did he do there?

Beersheba was the southernmost tip of the land of Canaan. During the days of the kings of Israel, a way to describe the length of the land was to say, "From Dan to Beersheba." It would be like an American saying from Maine to Florida. Whenever I return to Michigan, I have a longing to drive by 3640 Pontiac Lake Road, the former home of my grandparents. I sit on the side of the road and let my mind run through the halls of memories of all that once happened at that location. Beersheba was full of memories for Jacob.

What took place at Beersheba and to whom in the following passages:

Genesis 21:33:

Genesis 26:23-24:

Beersheba had been the place where Abraham, Jacob's grandfather, had called on the name of the Lord and Isaac, Jacob's father, had received the same covenantal promise that Jehovah had made to Abraham that all his offspring would be blessed. It was entirely appropriate that Jacob visit this sacred spot before he left Canaan alive. It was both merciful and loving for the Lord to choose that time and that place to visit Jacob, now known by God as Israel.

This was Jacob's seventh and last visitation from God. After reading about Jacob's first visitation by God in Genesis 28:10-22, compare and contrast this passage with Genesis 46:1-7:

Similarities

Differences

In both situations, Jacob was leaving his home for the unknown. But the most marked difference this time was in who sought whom out first. The Jacob of Genesis 28 was a self-assured, cocky trickster who lived mostly by his wits. There was no sacrifice to God as there was in Genesis 46. Jacob had been educated by the school of suffering which had revised the conditional attitude he once had of making the God of his fathers his own. An old man had learned to bow his knee as a gracious God stooped down to bless the one who had called on Him.

What four promises did God make to Jacob in Genesis 46:3-4?

Change without God's blessing is terrifying. Change with God's blessing need not be terrifying when we follow the commands of Philippians 4:6-7. What steps are we to follow in these verses and what is our promised reward? How does this promise specifically comfort you right now?

Let's continue reading Genesis 46:8-27. Circle the number of Jacob's family:

thirty seventy one hundred five hundred

What promise did Abraham receive about his descendants in Genesis 12:1-3?

Change without God's blessing is terrifying.

The obstacles to the fulfillment of this promise seemed impossible when the promise was given because Abraham had a barren wife. After waiting for twenty-five years, a son named Isaac was born to Abraham at age one hundred. Surely God would now bless Isaac, the son of promise, with many children! Isaac and Rebekah suffered through twenty years of infertility before their twin boys, Esau and Jacob, were born. Esau despised his birthright. God rejected Esau and chose Jacob to continue the promise given Abraham and Isaac before him. There was only one person in each of the three generations of this family through whom God would fulfill His promise. Jacob went to Egypt without knowing how God would fulfill the promise He had made to him at Beersheba, but Jacob went with God's blessing after offering sacrifices to the Lord. Peace that passed understanding was his.

Let's continue reading Genesis 46:28-34 and answer the following questions:

Which family member reached Joseph first and why?

The next two questions are important to remember for tomorrow's lesson:
What location did the family go to in Egypt?

What specific instructions did Joseph give to his brothers as to what they were to say to Pharaoh when they were presented before him (verses 33-34)?

The journey to Egypt had been a series of full circle moments for Jacob as he once again encountered the God of his fathers, Abraham and Isaac. There are some full circle moments we never expect to experience. One such moment awaited an elderly, feeble man as he watched the dust flying behind the chariot of the second in command of all Egypt as it made its approach. The son who had been lost to Jacob for over twenty years had unexpectedly been restored to him. Surely Jacob understood in that moment what he had fought to fully surrender to for so many years: that Jehovah was the God of Abraham, Isaac, *and* Jacob. I cannot imagine the charged emotional atmosphere as Joseph, the viceroy of Egypt, became Joseph the beloved son once again as he fell on Jacob's neck and let loose a floodgate of tears on his daddy's shoulder.

What does Psalm 56:8 tell us that God does with our tears?

Write out your two most important questions which you are waiting for answers from God here:

One day, my sweet sister, you and I will see that in those times in which we felt utterly abandoned that we were believing a lie. We will know that our God was there with us through every painful experience. We will understand fully how beloved we always were to our great and awesome God. We, too, will have a full circle moment as this distorted mirror we currently see through is shattered forever and we will fully know why even as we are fully known.

We will then understand the plan of glory.

Now we see but a poor reflection as in a mirror; then we shall see face to face. Now I know in part; then I shall know fully, even as I am fully known.
– 1 Corinthians 13:12

Day Three – The Benefits of Wisdom

I live in the Music City where new, aspiring artists come with a dream to make it big in this town. A very few eventually see those dreams come true, but not usually without paying some dues performing mundane tasks like waiting tables to cover the rent for long years before their music has radio play. There really is no overnight success story here. Most people will tell you that talent is not the reason one person makes it big and ten thousand others do not. Most have tremendous talent. The true reason for someone's success is usually due to who he/she knew at a pivotal moment in time.

Have you ever been the recipient of the favor of someone because of a mutual friend (e.g. getting a job interview, being part of a project, being given a role of leadership, etc.)?

What does Proverbs 22:1 declare to be better than riches? Circle one:

Obedient children   No debt or creditors   A good name

From his first position as a slave in Potiphar's house, Joseph had proven that he was a person who could be trusted. After a false accusation of rape landed him in prison, Joseph continued to build a stellar reputation with the prison warden. The prison warden, like Potiphar, did not concern himself with anything while Joseph was in charge. As second only to Pharaoh in power, Joseph had found great favor as a brilliant and just administrator.

What reward in Proverbs 3:4 comes from a life of love and faithfulness in Proverbs 3:3?

Joseph would have known where the best land was in all of Egypt. What knowledge did Joseph have that the brothers and even Jacob did not fully understand in Genesis 45:5?

After reading Genesis 47:1-6, list the specific steps Joseph took to secure land in Goshen for his brothers and his father:

Did you notice that Joseph never used his position to demand what he wanted Pharaoh to do for his family? Ladies, humility and patience will always get us so much farther than manipulation and entitlement. Why? Because when we humble ourselves under God's mighty hand, He will lift us up in due time (1 Peter 5:6). Joseph did not use his power for position or personal gain. Joseph continued to trust the One whom Joseph was truly serving. He had seen God raise him from prison as a slave and exalt him to the second highest position in the land in one day. Surely God could handle a real estate transaction! I have so much to learn from Joseph!

What situation are you tempted to manipulate that you know God wants you to trust Him for?

Make no mistake, my dear friend! Living to please Christ is going to cost us greatly in our own desires, but there is no better way to live! What a huge relief it is to me to not have to be in the driver's seat of my life, stressing over my future.

Let's continue reading Genesis 47:7-12 and answer the following questions:

Humility and patience will always get us so much farther than manipulation and entitlement.

Who presented Jacob before Pharaoh (verse 7)?

What did Jacob do to Pharaoh (verse 7)?

The very young and the very old are allowed privileges that those in between are not given. Both can speak their minds and not be judged for their words or go places which are prohibited for others. I remember watching a movie which chronicled a former African American slave's life whose one hundred two year life span allowed her to see the beginning of the civil rights' activities in the south. One of the last scenes of the movie was of this elderly woman leaning heavily on a cane, slowly and deliberately approaching a water fountain with a sign above it that read *White Only*. Although she had to pass a group of menacing white men to get a drink of water, she drank from the very fountain which would have gotten her beaten had she been younger. Her age and her frailty were her safeguards even among those who hated her.

Jacob's age gave him license to do what even Joseph could not do – talk to Pharaoh as an equal. There was no bowing before Pharaoh on Jacob's part. His gray head earned him respect from the ruler of the then known world that one hundred thirty years of life brought into the throne room that day.

What did Pharaoh ask Jacob in verse 8?

How did Jacob reply to this question? Why do you think he responded this way?

The truth is, my dear friend, being elderly is not synonymous with being wise. A life of conditional surrender to God's plan for our lives will never produce happy memories. God had met Jacob at Bethel long before Leah, Rachel, Bilhah, and Zilpah and twelve sons were in his life (see Genesis 28:20-22). Jacob had suffered the loss of family relationships from the very beginning through deception of his own and through being deceived.

What does Proverbs 19:23 promise us?

Do you believe that Jacob now realized this emotional state in his own life? Why or why not?

A life of conditional surrender to God's plan for our lives will never produce happy memories.

What kind of sins are we perpetuating in our lives that would keep us from fully receiving a life of contentment and peace? Does jealousy, hatred, anger, or bitterness toward others or in our families hoard any room for possible contentment or peace? How tragic to be like Jacob and look back at our lives with deep regret and sorrow for what never was and could have been had we learned to fully surrender our pain and ask God to use it for His glory. At the end of our lives are we going to see that our legacy was withholding forgiveness, deceiving others, and refusing to heal – sins which stole from us the abundant life Jesus promised is ours!

What amazing act did Joseph do for his brothers in Genesis 47:12?

What was happening to the Egyptians and Canaanites in contrast to Jacob's family in verse 13?

List the steps the Egyptians took to provide for themselves in verses 14-26:

I grew up in a country ruled by the iron grip of a cruel dictator who used the billions of dollars given to his country in aid money to line his own pockets. Joseph did not use power to destroy and impoverish. He was a true steward – protecting the interests of his king while maintaining the health and dignity of his subjects.

What was the response of the Egyptians to Joseph's administrative decisions during the famine in verse 25?

Let's conclude our study today by reading Genesis 47:27-31.

If we are faithless, he will remain faithful, for he cannot disown himself.
2 Timothy 2:13

God does not forsake His own. Let me say that again: God does not forsake His own. Not because of us, but because He cannot be unfaithful to Himself. God had made a covenantal promise with Abraham, Isaac, and also to Jacob. Although Jacob had faltered on his end and had lied to others, the God who had made the promise to be Jacob's God never promised something that He would not fulfill. In the middle of famine, God continued to bless a fledgling family of seventy bruised and scarred family members through whom He would one day bring His beloved Son to earth. The pain and bitterness that were a part of Jacob's legacy were never part of God's will for him. But our God will reign supreme over the worst pain we have endured and will remain faithful for the saving of many lives if we will allow Him.

God does not forsake His own. Let me say that again: God does not forsake His own.

What promise had God made to Jacob in Genesis 46:4?

How was Joseph involved in this promise (Genesis 47:29-30)?

I can relate to Jacob on a small level. I spent eight of the most formative years of my childhood in Congo. Although I love Africa, and it will always be in my blood, I love my own country of America best. My flag is the star spangled banner. My roots are here. It is one of the greatest privileges I have been given to be a citizen of a country that was founded on Judeo-Christian principles. While Congo is my home away from home, the United States of America is my true home. Although seventeen years had passed since he had left his home in Canaan, Jacob would never be an Egyptian. The God of his fathers, who had appeared to Abraham and Isaac, had assured Jacob that his final resting place would not be in the land of the Nile, but in the land of Canaan. Jacob had seen the power of Jehovah to bring about the impossible by not only making his descendants thrive in a foreign land during a world wide famine, but by allowing his long lost son, Joseph, to be the instrument through which these blessings had come.

Life had been long and difficult for Jacob, but a contented old man had much to be grateful for as he leaned upon his staff and worshiped the God of his fathers who had now become his own. Can we see through the study of the Word of God, my dear sister, that conditional surrender and a lifetime of regrets are no way to live? I pray that we will be wise enough, while there is still time for our Redeemer to restore what the locusts have eaten (Joel 2:25), to make Jacob's God our God, too.

I pray that we will be wise enough, while there is still time for our Redeemer to restore what the locusts have eaten (Joel 2:25), to make Jacob's God our God, too.

Day Four – A Do Over Moment

I have been blessed to be the daughter of a great man who has followed hard after Jesus since he lost his brother at the age of sixteen. My father has given me the most incredible gift anyone can receive – the gift of faithful love to my mother for almost fifty years and the gift of unconditional love for each of his four children and our families. I have always known that I could call him at 3:00 a.m. and he would drop everything to come to my aid.

My parents made sure that we saw each other every four to six weeks when I attended boarding school four hundred miles away from our mission station in Congo. Dad would take my sister and me out to Ani's, our favorite Chinese restaurant in downtown Kinshasa, where we would feast on an eight-course meal. We could forget, if just for a little while, that most of our lives were spent apart during those years. Like so many other missionary children, living away from our parents was part of life on the mission field. It was a hard sacrifice for all of us to be absent from each other's daily lives.

I spent four years in boarding school away from my parents, but I saw them every month or two for a week. I cannot imagine what it must have been like for Joseph to adjust to the reality that his family was once again accessible to him. The hope of seeing his father's face again must have given him a reason to live on many a dark day as he adjusted to a life he was forced to live as a slave. By the time he came face-to-face with his brothers who did not recognize him, he must have wondered if Jacob was even alive.

I have been blessed to be the daughter of a great man who has followed hard after Jesus since he lost his brother at the age of sixteen.

There is a sad realization which I have been stunned with this last year as my eldest prepares for his first year of high school: I cannot turn back the clock. I had three children in three and a half years. I remember the days when they were little as being long ones, but now the clock has suddenly accelerated and now I am counting the years I have left with my son on one hand before he is a man. The days of their toddler, preschool and early elementary years were long, but I now know that the years are short.

What did Moses implore of God in Psalm 90:12?

How is time passing for you right now? Circle the best answer:

Slow as molasses   Just about right   Flying by too fast

Explain the reason for your choice above:

Jacob and Joseph could never relive the years they had lived apart in Joseph's life from age seventeen to thirty-nine when their reunion most likely took place (Joseph rose to power at age thirty and recognized his brothers two years into the famine after the seven years of abundance). To put this in

perspective, I thought we would chronicle our own life story at the same ages as Scripture gives for Joseph at different points we have studied in his story.

Where were you and who were the most important people in your life at:

Age 17:

Age 30:

Age 39:

My current age:

The only thing we can truly count on is change, even from year to year.

We are not even the same people that we once were! None of the most important people in my life, besides my family, at age seventeen and thirty are in my life on a regular basis today. Even in the four years since I left my thirties, my close circle of friends has changed somewhat. The only thing we can truly count on is change, even from year to year.

Over twenty years had been lost between father and son, but today's passage is an intimate look at the abiding love Jacob and Joseph had for each other. God had granted them seventeen years together in Egypt. Jacob was now nearing the sunset of his life and desired to talk one-on-one with his beloved Joseph. Alone.

Our passage for today is Genesis 48. Let's read verses 1-7 together and ponder the following questions:

Why did Joseph go to see Jacob and who accompanied him there?

Joseph would have known the information Jacob talked with him about in verses 3-4 and verse 7. Why do you think Jacob was recalling these events?

My grandfather was diagnosed with Alzheimer's disease at the age of eighty-eight, eighteen months after my grandmother died. Although so many of his memories were gone or confused, he continued to talk about my grandmother and events that had happened decades before. His mind continued to cling to memories of when he was in the prime of his life. Jacob continued to love the one woman who had always been the love of his life, Rachel, who had died over fifty years earlier. (Did you notice that none of the other three mothers of his sons were mentioned?)

Sometimes, ladies, God gives us a do-over moment. Unconfessed sin and unresolved guilt can steal these precious opportunities from us. Matthew 5:8 tells us: "Blessed are the pure in heart, for they will see God." I want to seize on every opportunity He may bring to redeem something in my life. I must be pure before Him to be able to see those God-given opportunities.

A do over moment comes to our attention when we realize that we have been in a similar situation before, but we now understand we have the opportunity to see a different outcome. After reading Genesis 48:8-20, let's compare and contrast the blessing Jacob gave to his grandsons with the one he deceived Isaac to give him in Genesis 27.

Compare and contrast the following verses:

Genesis 48:8-9 with Genesis 27:18-19:

Genesis 48:10 with Genesis 27:1, 25-26:

Genesis 48:13-14 with Genesis 27:27:

Genesis 48:15-16 with Genesis 27:28-29:

Genesis 48:18-20 with Genesis 27:38-40:

A do over moment comes to our attention when we realize that we have been in a similar situation before, but we now understand we have the opportunity to see a different outcome.

The first week of this study we uncovered sinful patterns in our families. We in the western culture cannot understand how powerful the blessing of the firstborn was in biblical times. The firstborn received the double portion of the father's inheritance by law. God had made a covenant with each of the patriarchs starting with Joseph's great grandfather, Abraham. Isaac received the blessing from Abraham. Jacob received the blessing from Isaac through deception.

My question to us, ladies, is this: What would have happened if Abraham, Isaac, and Jacob had trusted God to bring about His own perfect plan in His own perfect timing in their families? Let's examine this a little more closely.

Each generation's lack of trust in God in the area of their families brought great devastation and bitterness. Abraham and Sarah decided to "help" God by building a family through Sarah's maidservant. Isaac received the covenantal blessing. Ishmael was sent away with his mother. We don't have to wonder if there was any animosity about this show of favoritism of Abraham toward Isaac. We only need to pick up a newspaper or turn on the television to read about the millennia-old conflict that continues to the present day between the Arabs (descendants of Ishmael) and the nation of Israel (descendants of Isaac).

The sons of Isaac and Rebekah did not have to wonder if they were judging correctly that one parent favored one brother over the other. Scripture is clear that the favoritism in Esau and Jacob's childhood home was blatant. Rebekah and Jacob cooked up a scheme involving a goat with the goal of stealing the blessing that should have gone to Esau according to Isaac's plan.

What does Proverbs 21:30 tell us?

We say we trust God with our mouths, but our actions may tell a different story. If we actually believed that Proverbs 21:30 was the truth, how much of the pain we carry today from our manipulation could we have been spared? Jacob may have received the blessing, but at what cost? He had to flee for his life from Esau who wanted to kill him. Jacob probably never saw his mother and co-conspirator, Rebekah, alive again, and one of the most dreaded moments he had ever had was meeting up with his estranged brother again. The deceptive lifestyle Jacob adopted before he ever left home created such a wake of devastation in his own family of twelve sons that could have been avoided had he let God be God.

The use of power for Joseph did not mean the oppression of others. It meant the saving and redemption of many lives.

When Jacob blessed his two grandsons, there was no deceit or animosity. Both boys received the same blessing, even though Ephraim would be more influential in the lives of the future Israelites. The blessing brought unity between not only Joseph's sons, but the twelve sons of Jacob who would one day make up the twelve tribes of the nation of Israel.

Joseph, the one who had the most to forgive, had no hidden agenda or deception as his sons received his grandfather's blessing. He had not jockeyed for position or slandered his brothers, although he could have easily done that with the power that he had over them. But the use of power for Joseph did not mean the oppression of others. It meant the saving and redemption of many lives. The fires of severe trial and suffering in Joseph had provided a do over moment for his entire family. Joseph, of anyone we have studied in the book of Genesis had the most justifiable reasons for not forgiving. But by his obedience, he broke the chain of jealousy, bitterness, and hatred that had visited every generation of his family for four generations. Joseph saw what I am begging the Holy Spirit to show us: that God, through Joseph's staunch devotion to making the God of Abraham, Isaac, and Jacob his God as a member of the fourth generation of his family, would do a new work in the lives of the fifth generation and for a thousand after because Joseph loved God!

Are you and I willing to be like Joseph? Even if you and I have come from families in which destruction has reigned as far back as we can remember – divorce, addictions, infidelity, hatred toward God and His Word – we can be the first generation of the new story that God wants to write for our families!

It will cost us everything in our natural desires, my darling friend, to deny ourselves the right to seek revenge on those who have hurt us so badly. But the payoff is beyond what we could possibly imagine. God never forgets - never.

As we close, let's read this amazing promise and cry out to the God who is sovereign over all that has happened to you to help you see its realization in your own life:

Then you will call, and the LORD will answer;
you will cry for help, and he will say: Here am I.
"If you do away with the yoke of oppression,
with the pointing finger and malicious talk,
and if you spend yourselves in behalf of the hungry
and satisfy the needs of the oppressed,
then your light will rise in the darkness,
and your night will become like the noonday.
The LORD will guide you always;
he will satisfy your needs in a sun-scorched land
and will strengthen your frame.
You will be like a well-watered garden,
like a spring whose waters never fail.
Your people will rebuild the ancient ruins
and will raise up the age-old foundations;
you will be called Repairer of Broken Walls,
Restorer of Streets with Dwellings.
–Isaiah 58:9-12

It will cost us everything in our natural desires, my darling friend, to deny ourselves the right to seek revenge on those who have hurt us so badly.

As we close, I wanted to include the prayer of my heart:

Lord Jesus, please help me to start anew in my family so that I, like Joseph, can one day be known as a repairer of broken walls and a restorer of streets with dwellings in my family. Empower me to do what is impossible without You....

May I forgive those as You have forgiven me. Let me seize this do over moment.

Day Five – What is Due Me

After years of procrastinating, Rob and I finally got around to making out a will to remove any doubt about where we wanted our minor children and assets to go should we both suddenly be taken from this life. I never knew preparing to die while each of us still enjoyed good health was such a complicated process! There were decisions we were asked to make that had never crossed either one of our minds, like what music did we want played at our funeral and where we wanted our final earthly resting place to be. The experience was both surreal and sobering as we came face-to-face with our own mortality.

Dysfunctional families spend a great deal of time and energy trying to avoid one another. Some of us have family members that we dread seeing. There are usually only two occasions that consistently bring estranged family members together - weddings and funerals.

Joseph and Jacob had shared a tender moment alone with Joseph's sons in yesterday's lesson, but today we are going to get a glimpse into the mind of Jacob and the future of these twelve sons who would birth the longest lasting nation in the history of the world - the Jewish people. Isn't it incredible that a perfect God would choose such an imperfect family through whom to bring His own sinless Son, Jesus Christ?

We may have come to believe the lie that there is no reward for trying to obey Him as we do not seek revenge on our own.

How does this observation give you hope about your own family and about God's power despite what has happened in the past between family members?

Although Jacob lay dying, he was still the head of his family. At his request, every one of his twelve sons – including the one who was second in command of all Egypt – came to his bedside to hear Jacob's final blessing over each son's life. The words we are about to read coming from Jacob's mouth were not his own. They were words of prophecy to reward not only the intended son, but also his descendants. Some of us are struggling with the seeming injustice of having to forgive because it seems as though our offender has gotten away with the sin he or she has committed against us. God seems to have overlooked what this person has done to us. And we may have come to believe the lie that there is no reward for trying to obey Him as we do not seek revenge on our own.

What does Galatians 6:8-9 assure us is the truth?

There is a law of harvest going on continually, my dear sister. If we have sown deeds of obedience to please the Holy Spirit, there is going to be a day when God, the righteous Judge will reward us for what we have done. He has seen everything. He knows the motive behind the action and He will judge according to His perfect justice.

Genesis 49 is going to make this principle of harvest very real. We are going to take these verses in two parts. Let's read Genesis 49:1-28.

What was the long-lasting consequence of Reuben's sin in verse 4 (see Genesis 35:22) as well as the consequence of Simeon and Levi's acts of revenge against the Shechemites in verse 7 (see Genesis 34:25-29)?

Just as Reuben had failed to be able to persuade his brothers to not harm Joseph as they sold him as a slave, the descendants of Reuben would not excel as people of influence in Israel in the generations to come. The descendants of Simeon were eventually absorbed by the tribe of Judah (see 1 Chronicles 4:24-33). The descendants of Levi were the one tribe who did not receive a land inheritance like the other eleven tribes did. They were scattered throughout the tribes. God was not through with Levi. The one who would eventually take the descendants of these twelve brothers up out of slavery under the Egyptians in a glorious deliverance was a Hebrew baby born from this tribe – Moses. The Levites were also the ones whom God chose as priests to serve Him in the temple.

Judah was the next in line. How would you characterize Judah's blessing compared to Reuben, Simeon, and Levi's? Does this surprise you?

Of all the brothers, Judah had changed the most since our early introductions to him. Judah was the mastermind behind Joseph's selling and his shady moral choices with Tamar. My dear sister, our God does not judge as we do! What do we do when we have a track record of moral failure and a history of destructive decisions? The latter half of Judah's life is proof that God does not reject those who stand broken before Him.

What do the following Scriptures reveal to us about what God delights in that Judah accomplished in his actions toward Benjamin?

Proverbs 10:12:

John 15:12-14:

1 Peter 4:8:

What had inspired Judah to step out from the rest of his brothers with knocking knees before the one Judah believed to be the viceroy of Egypt and beg Joseph to make him a slave instead of Benjamin? Genuine anguish over the thought of the despair it would cause the little brother he had promised to bring back to the father who had never really shown Judah that kind of devotion in return. Judah was willing to lay down his own life for Benjamin. My darling sister, is it worth our time and effort to love, to lay down our own expectations for love with someone who may not love us back the way we want them to? Yes! Because the One who loved us enough to lay down His life for you and me will be the righteous Judge who will one day reward us for the love we continued to show to those who could not or would not love us back. Love, my dear friend, love even though it causes such suffering to do so. Your heavenly Father knows what you are doing and is delighted with you.

What Genesis 29:35 give as the meaning of Judah's name? Circle one:

Praise the Lord Son of my right hand Son of my sorrow

Aren't we so thankful that God can take a messed up life and bring Himself praise and glory through that life? Judah finally had lived up to his name.

Aren't we so thankful that God can take a messed up life and bring Himself praise and glory through that life?

Genesis 49:13-21, 27 gives us the only other individualized information we have about these seven sons from four different mothers. As often happens in a large group, there are those individuals who stand out and those who recede into the background. Which one of the six blessings given here would you have most liked to receive and why?

What did Jacob recognize as the source of Joseph's ability to be fruitful and stand strong against the bitterness of the archers (perhaps the ten older brothers who stood with him around Jacob's bed) who attacked him in verses 24-25?

Verse 26 in the English Standard Version (ESV) reads like this:

The blessings of your father
are mighty beyond the blessings of my parents,
up to the bounties of the everlasting hills.
May they be on the head of Joseph,
and on the brow of him who was set apart from his brothers.

You and I might live and die without seeing blessings like this for our faithfulness to God by reacting like Joseph did. What does Isaiah 49:4 reassure us is coming on the other side of eternity?

My dad used to say a little phrase to my siblings and me as we were growing up:

We have only one life, 'twill soon be past; only what's done for Christ will last.

One day God is going to call all of us to account to judge us for what we did in the body while we lived and breathed the air of earth. I cannot believe that Joseph regretted granting forgiveness as his beloved father breathed his last breath. And, my darling sister, you and I will not regret the forgiveness we gave, even if we did not see reconciliation happen in our situations. Listen to what is ahead of us!

If you love those who love you, what credit is that to you? Even 'sinners' love those who love them. And if you do good to those who are good to you, what credit is that to you? Even 'sinners' do that. And if you lend to those from whom you expect repayment, what credit is that to you? Even 'sinners' lend to 'sinners,' expecting to be repaid in full. But love your enemies, do good to them, and lend to them without expecting to get anything back. Then your reward will be great, and you will be sons of the Most High, because he is kind to the ungrateful and wicked. Be merciful, just as your Father is merciful.

Luke 6:32-36

What striking fact about the blessings does Genesis 49:28 point out? Circle one:

They were fair and appropriate Jacob showed favoritism
Some were rejected

If God spoke justly through a father who at times was prone to favoritism, we can be assured that when He judges us and those we would like to judge, His judgments will be fair and appropriate also.

Let's conclude by reading Genesis 49:29-33.

After reading Genesis 17:7-8 and Genesis 46:3-4, why do you think that Jacob was so explicit in his instructions to his sons about where he desired to be buried?

And so the weary pilgrim ended his journey of one hundred forty-seven years and breathed his last with the faces of his twelve sons all together as Jacob's eyelids closed forever on earth. He had given his final blessing and instruction. The brothers had come together as a family unit to their dying father's side. Peace prevailed – for now.

Forgiveness takes one person. Reconciliation takes both parties coming together to pay the costly price of being restored to each other. A question that had lurked beneath the surface for seventeen years was about to explode in the near future. With their father now dead, what was the true status of the brothers' relationship to Joseph?

Had reconciliation truly occurred between Joseph and his brothers or not? That was the question. That really is the question for all of us to ask in our own struggle with forgiveness.

Had reconciliation truly occurred between Joseph and his brothers or not? That was the question.

Reconciliation's Requirements

Have you ever left out a key ingredient to a recipe? I remember the stint of baking bread from scratch my sister and I took on to sell in Congo to make some spending money. Looking back, my heart warms at my mother's support of our endeavors (many of them miserable failures!) as we used our pantry's limited resources. Nicol and I quickly learned that some of the ingredients called for in the recipe could not be substituted or skimped on in their measurements. Flour and yeast had to be existent in the right proportions or the loaf of bread would turn out to be inedible.

For reconciliation to occur, key ingredients or necessary requirements must be met between two hurt people. Forgiveness can be granted by one person; reconciliation cannot. Both the offender and the offended must commit to the, sometimes, agonizing task of healing with the requirements we will look at this week. We will look closely at the final chapter of Genesis to discern if reconciliation truly occurred between the brothers and Joseph during their many years of life together in Egypt.

As we bring our study to a close, I wanted us to honestly ask ourselves if we are willing to participate by joining God in the ministry of reconciliation He has granted to us through Jesus Christ.

Once you were alienated from God and were enemies in your minds because of your evil behavior. But now he has reconciled you by Christ's physical body through death to present you holy in his sight, without blemish and free from accusation–if you continue in your faith, established and firm, not moved from the hope held out in the gospel. This is the gospel that you heard and that has been proclaimed to every creature under heaven, and of which I, Paul, have become a servant.

Colossians 3:21-23

This week we will examine reconciliation's difficult requirements in a relationship where trust had once been trampled. Forgiveness is not an option for us as followers of Jesus Christ, my precious friend! In evaluating our own responsibility in reconciling with others, we must remember how merciful our God has been to us through the blood of His Son, Jesus Christ. We are no longer enemies with the One who has given us the ministry of reconciliation. Our time together will end with a glorious hope for all those who have called on the Name of Jesus Christ for salvation.

Day 1 – A Love That Surpasses Knowledge

I attended my son's eighth grade graduation this last May and felt my stomach tighten with a certain amount of dread as the familiar tune of "Pomp and Circumstance" filled the gym where the ceremony was held. Those musical bars signal endings to me as well as beginnings in which I can no longer take part. Perhaps what I fear most is the goodbye that always accompanies the song. The end of each school year as a missionary kid in the Congo included a graduation that removed people from my life forever. Unlike many of my friends that did not grow up overseas, I did not live in a place where college students returned every Christmas and summer to their hometown. I have never seen some of my friends since the day they graduated and left Congo for their new lives after high school. I didn't know how to give my heart halfway. I loved in a way in which my heart bled with every good-bye I said. I shed more tears in the month of June than in all the other months of the year combined. I knew as I watched my friends walk across the stage to receive their diplomas that a chapter of my life was closed, never to be reopened again. And, as the one not yet graduating, I was left behind to face the forever altered normal state that had once been. I am a basket case at graduations – even eighth grade graduations when no one is leaving!

One day, death will be no more. There will be no more crying, no health problems, no mourning for we will live fully in God's presence where those difficulties will no longer exist.

What is the last great enemy that will be conquered according to Revelation 20:14?

I have not experienced the loss of a parent. Although my parents have followed hard after Jesus their entire lives, I dread the sting of death and the inevitable, but relatively short, good-bye that will follow them going home to be with Jesus.

One day, death will be no more. There will be no more crying, no health problems, no mourning for we will live fully in God's presence where those difficulties will no longer exist. We will look on our Redeemer's face who will Himself wipe away our tears (see Revelation 21:3-4). That glad day is coming for all of us who have made Jesus Christ our Savior, but until He comes back to take us to be with Him, we will come face-to-face with the cruel truth that death is a part of every life that breathes on this earth.

We have come to the last chapter in Genesis, the book of beginnings. After Jacob had blessed each of his sons, he breathed his last. Let's read Genesis 50:1-14. Circle the names of those who wept over Jacob in verse 1:

All twelve sons Joseph and Benjamin Joseph alone

Why do you think Scripture only records his name here?

Can a scarred heart be unmoved by what should bring tears? Have you any life experience that would help to validate this thought?

I watched a news program during my college years that is burned in my memory about babies who had either been abandoned or had no living parents, lying in cribs in an orphanage in Romania. The eerie sound of silence was commented on by the reporter who was aghast at the lack of attention these children received day after day. The orphanage worker told him that the babies had learned that their crying would not get them the comfort that they needed. There were simply too many children with too many needs for the few workers to adequately handle. Row after row of cribs contained babies who had shut down emotionally and stared out of vacant eyes. I sobbed through the whole story and wanted to jump on the next plane to rescue as many as I could.

What does 1 Peter 4:8 reveal to us? Do you think the ten older brothers felt this from their father?

I know that Scripture simply may not have included the tears of the brothers in the last chapter of Genesis (which may well have come during Jacob's final words over them), but it is striking to me that the beloved son of Jacob could weep so affectionately over his father even after all the years of separation between them. If our children know that we love them, we cover over a multitude of sins in our parenting. If the opposite is true, our sins will be glaring to them in the end and may prevent them from feeling the grief that they should feel. God has been convicting me so greatly in the area of telling my children **daily** that I love them deeply. I can get so busy and self-absorbed and not have a clue as to what lies Satan is feeding them about being unloved because I do not take the time to sit down and ask.

A heart who does not believe he/she is loved has a cavernous hole that can never be filled.

A heart who does not believe he/she is loved has a cavernous hole that can never be filled. We can make such destructive decisions when we do not understand or accept how deeply loved we are by God and instead look to fallible human beings or ourselves to try to fill the desperate need our hearts have to be loved unconditionally.

After reading Romans 5:1-5, list in order what the benefits of suffering bring to Christ-followers:

What does the apostle Paul tell us that the last benefit listed in verse 4 will do for us and why in verse 5?

How important is hope in our lives? Without hope, there is no purpose in our pain. If we remain ignorant of the benefits of suffering and the beautiful and miraculous transformation that God offers to us through our darkest trials, we will not be able to grasp the love that the Holy Spirit desires to lavish on us. Without suffering, we will not understand the fullness of God's love and mercy for us because suffering presses us into the image of Christ. We will not be permitted to attain the incomparable riches which God would have for us that cannot be found on any other pathway than the one of suffering. We will not see the depth to which God is willing to visit us at our greatest emotional anguish and become our Redeemer. We will not become like Him through any other means because we are slaves to sin, even after we become His followers (see Romans 7:14-18).

What were the biblical authors' responses to what suffering had produced in them in following Scriptures?

Psalm 31:7-8:

James 1:2:

1 Peter 1:6-7:

2 Timothy 4:6-7:

If we remain ignorant of the benefits of suffering and the beautiful and miraculous transformation that God offers to us through our darkest trials, we will not be able to grasp the love that the Holy Spirit desires to lavish on us.

Circle the reaction(s) you most often default to when suffering comes to you:

God is punishing me.

I anticipate the opportunity to see how Jesus is going to change me.

I panic over how I am going to handle and get through this.

Joseph knew he was deeply loved by his father, Jacob. I believe his father's love gave Joseph comfort during the years he spent as a slave and a prisoner. But an earthly father's love is not enough to sustain us through the darkest hours we face if we do not believe that our heavenly Father has a beneficial purpose to transform us through our suffering.

Joseph's ten older brothers did not have the security of Jacob's love. I believe that profoundly affected their ability to fight against the sinful desires that overtook them in their actions toward Joseph. What do we do if our life experience includes deep insecurities that stem from feeling unloved by those who had a lasting influence on our lives (e.g. parents, siblings, extended family members)?

The apostle Paul understood that we humans tend to think what has happened to us is truth. If we were loved deeply, we believe we are worthy of love. If we were not loved as we should have been, we can carry wounds that prevent us from accepting love from others or even from God Himself.

After reading Ephesians 3:16-19, what did Paul specifically pray for the church at Ephesus in verse 19?

Take a look back at your family tree in Week one, Day two's homework. Without seeing these sins through the redemptive lens of Scripture, that is your truth because it is your life experience. What God's magnificent, healing Word reveals is that your sin-tainted life experiences. are not His truth, which trumps the lies of our "truth." My darling friend, you and I need to pray *every day* that the Holy Spirit will silence the voice of the enemy that shouts to us that our God does not love us! That is a lie from the pit of hell. But our life experience will threaten to have us deny the truth of Scripture which is that God's love for us is complete and eternal. We can never do anything which will make Him not love us anymore, unlike a fickle, fallen human being's limited capacity for unconditional love. You and I are accepted in the Beloved (Ephesians 1:6, KJV), not because of anything we have done or not done, but because of God's faithfulness to Himself and His Word!

Scripture does not record Joseph ever experiencing a visitation from God like the three patriarchs before him received. Perhaps, though, Joseph was the recipient of an experience far better. Joseph knew God spoke to and through him in dreams and revelations. Joseph knew that God was with him in prison. Joseph experienced God's favor. Joseph watched God do the impossible as He lifted him from the pit of suffering to an exalted place of honor. A visitation can be blurred with doubt. There is nothing more powerful than when head knowledge that Jesus is mighty to save becomes our own heart knowledge in the deep valley of trouble as we watch our God come to rescue us in a way that only He could. No one can take that treasure away from us that He gave us in the darkness.

The love of Joseph's God covered a multitude of sins that had been committed against him by those who should have loved him.

I believe forgiveness was given by Joseph to his brothers before the brothers left Canaan the first time to go to Egypt to buy grain for their starving households. Joseph settled deep issues with God about his value even as he was devalued in the eyes of a vindictive, would-be seductress in a prison cell he did not deserve. He had not used his power or position to crush his brothers or make their families suffer during the seventeen years since the seventy members of Jacob's family were reunited in Egypt from the land of Canaan. Joseph knew that the Lord was with him. The love of Joseph's God covered a multitude of sins that had been committed against him by those who should have loved him. The love of God can do the same for you and me, my precious friend, even if the forgiveness we offer to others is never accepted.

The passing of the person who holds a family together can expose the truth that things are not always as they appear. We are about to see what happens when someone does not settle reconciliation's first requirement of knowing how deeply they are loved by an infinite God. As Jacob's embalmed body was lain in the family tomb of Machpelah back in Canaan, a festering wound was about to reappear that would stun the brother who had loved in return for the hate that had been shown him. A fresh stab of grief in the heart of Joseph over this revelation would reveal doubt that reconciliation had ever really taken place between him and the his ten older brothers.

Day 2 – A Mutual Respect

Have you ever found yourself involved in something that you knew was a sin against God, but you also knew that no one would ever know the truth unless you confessed what you had done? You wrestled with the thought that your actions could easily be covered over with a feigned ignorance on your part of what you had done, but the guilt you felt over the circumstance let you know the truth that God understood your intent even if no one else did. I have been caught in this web before. I tried to minimize what I had done and reason my sin away. I can testify to the exhausting effort it cost me to cover up my sin when I did not want to confess to the person I had sinned against. The experience was horrid to go through.

What did David come to realize about his sin in Psalm 51:3-4?

What does guilt do to us according to the following Scriptures?

Psalm 32:4-5:

Psalm 51:8-9:

Psalm 90:8:

Let's read Genesis 50:15-17 and ponder the following questions: What fear arose in the brothers at the time of Jacob's death?

What would give you reason to believe that they did not believe that they were truly forgiven by Joseph?

Do you think the following phrase applies to the brothers: "We are most suspicious of others in areas of our own shortcomings?" Why?

What did the brothers do in response to their fear in Genesis 50:16-17?

Joseph and Jacob had time alone together in Genesis 48 when Jacob blessed Joseph's two young sons, Manasseh and Ephraim. Nowhere in their conversation does Scripture record Jacob being concerned about Joseph's treatment of his brothers after his death. If we scan Genesis 49, which recorded Jacob's deathbed blessings to his sons, nothing in Jacob's words indicate that Jacob doubted Joseph's forgiveness of his older brothers.

Crisis reveals in what or in whom we are putting our trust. Jacob's presence allowed the brothers to continue to receive the benefits of Joseph's forgiveness without having to fully acknowledge the weight of the sin they had committed against their brother. Now, without Jacob's presence in their lives, paranoia blinded them to the depth of Joseph's forgiveness.

What does 2 Corinthians 5:18 tell us we have been given through Christ? Fill in the blank:

The ministry of ______________________________________.

The greek word for reconciliation in this verse is from the root word *katallasso*. This is the definition Strong's Exhaustive Concordance gives for *katallasso*:

1) to change, exchange, as coins for others of equivalent value

- a) to reconcile (those who are at variance)
- b) return to favour with, be reconciled to one
- c) to receive one into favour[1]

Joseph and his brothers grew up in a family where all children were not treated equally. Jacob loved Joseph because he was the son of his most loved wife. Joseph had greater value in the eyes of his father because he belonged to Rachel. This created an environment of bitterness, hatred, and jealousy that destroyed any affection between Joseph and the sons of Leah, Bilhah and Zilpah. The brothers could not bring themselves to even speak kindly to Joseph (see Genesis 37:4) and plotted to murder him. Even though they did not physically kill him, the act of selling Joseph as a slave to the Ismaelites was like sending him to a living death.

How can we relate the following Scriptures to the brothers and what are the resulting effects of each passage?

Proverbs 10:18:

Hebrews 3:12-13:

Hebrews 12:15-16:

The brothers had to lie to Jacob to cover up the heinous act they had committed toward Joseph. Their hatred and bitterness turned into intense guilt that caused them to be blind to the relief that they could have received had they turned to Jehovah with their confession. Never once, in the whole story of Jacob's sons is their a moment of repentant confession before God. The brothers confessed there guilt in front of Joseph, thinking they were having a conversation among themselves in front of a stranger (see Genesis 42:21-23). Had they known that the stranger was Joseph, they would not have confessed! Nowhere recorded in Scripture is their confession to the One who could have granted them the forgiveness for which they so desperately longed.

What is the only relief for a guilty conscience according to Hebrews 10:22-23?

Only Jesus Christ has the power to forgive us and cleanse us completely of the guilt that may still be haunting us. A human being can forgive us, but can do nothing to remove the guilty conscience that we still may live with everyday.

What is the second requirement for reconciliation, my dear sister? Respect has to be mutually given and received by both parties. There must be safety where there was not safety before. There must be trust where trust has been trampled. There must be a commitment to do no harm against one another. Where there is a disparity in power, there is a great temptation for the one in the higher position to abuse that power. Although Joseph was the favored son of his father for all the years that he lived with his brothers in Canaan, all the brothers who sold him were much older than he. Joseph did not have a chance to escape their wicked plan to sell him – ten against one are unfair odds in anyone's estimation. Genesis 42:21 says, "They said to one another, 'Surely we are being punished because of our brother. We saw how distressed he was when he pleaded with us for his life, but we would not listen; that's why this distress has come upon us." By the time they sold Joseph into slavery, the brothers had long since ceased to see him as a person.

Only Jesus Christ has the power to forgive us and cleanse us completely of the guilt that may still be haunting us.

Glance back at Genesis 50:17. What was Joseph's reaction to the fabricated message of his brothers? Circle one:

He ordered them imprisoned. He wept. He sent for Judah.

The power had now swung in Joseph's favor in a way that made the brothers know that, with their father now dead, they were at Joseph's mercy for their survival. Joseph had shown profound respect for his brothers' dignity by showering on them lavish kindness during the seventeen years he had provided for them in the best land of Egypt. The brothers falsely believed that they were the recipients of Joseph's kindness solely because Jacob was alive.

Their lack of respect toward Joseph was profound and caused him to weep over the reality that his brothers remained blind to his forgiveness toward them long ago. Reconciliation between the two parties remained as distant as it ever had been.

Fill in the following blanks after looking up the Scriptures that accompany each one:

As an obedient follower of Christ, I am commanded in His Word to:

I am to love and do good to those who _______________ me (Luke 6:27-28).

In humility, I am to consider others as _______________ than myself (Phil. 2:3).

I am not to give the devil a _________________ related to sinful anger in my life (Ephesians 4:26-27).

My darling friend, how greatly do you and I stand in awe and respect due to Christ because of what He has done for us on the cross to cleanse us from our guilt? John 14:21 tells us that we show our love for Him by obeying what He commands. We are not given the option of obeying only what we want to obey in His Word. All of the above commands are death to my flesh. I do not want to obey, especially when the other party does not want to follow the requirements of reconciliation. I can stubbornly refuse to let Christ be Lord over the situation. I wonder if He wants to weep also when I refuse to treat His undeserved mercy and grace toward me with the profound gratitude I should. Like Joseph's brothers, I cower and want to run when my guilty conscience will not be silent. I allow Satan to tell me lies that the blood of Jesus is not powerful enough to cover my wickedness. I treat His grace with contempt and an unhealthy fear can take root that spirals into paranoia that He is someone waiting to zap me for my mistakes.

Even though we have received so great a salvation, we can become paralyzed in a pattern of sin and fear that makes us walk in defeat. There was a paralytic in the gospels whose friends were so desperate to get him to Jesus that they carried the young man on his mat and proceeded to tear off the roof tiles. They lowered their friend on the mat down into the house where Jesus was healing others. Jesus knew that the young man wanted physical healing, but his spiritual healing was an even greater need.

Even though we have received so great a salvation, we can become paralyzed in a pattern of sin and fear that makes us walk in defeat.

What did Jesus tell the paralyzed man before He healed his body in Luke 5:20?

Therefore, if anyone is in Christ, he is a new creation; the old has gone, the new has come! All this is from God, who reconciled us to himself through Christ and gave us the ministry of reconciliation: that God was reconciling the world to himself in Christ, not counting men's sins against them. And he has committed to us the message of reconciliation. 2 Corinthians 5:17-19

Friends, our sins are forgiven! Let's praise our Jesus for His authority to forgive us!

When we are convinced that God's love surpasses our human knowledge and experience (day one's requirement), we can more easily give and receive respect (day two's requirement) from the party that we need to forgive. Tomorrow's lesson will uncover one of the most critical requirements for us to be reconciled and restored with our offender.

Day 3 – A Repentant Confession

"Where there is no admission of guilt, healing and reconciliation are impossible." [2]

– Dr. Andrew Schmutzer

There are some very broken people walking around today in our churches. They do not want to cling to their brokenness, but they have come up against a serious impediment to their healing. They have been involved in some catastrophic relationships in which the abuse and wrongdoing that has happened to them has never been meaningfully acknowledged by the wrong-doer. Repentance (acknowledgement and a turning away from sin) has never been a part of the damaged relationship in which they were involved. Forgiveness only takes one person. Reconciliation takes two parties coming together with a sincere commitment to do what it takes to start the healing process.

Forgiveness only takes one person. Reconciliation takes two parties coming together with a sincere commitment to do what it takes to start the healing process.

Match the following Scriptures with the correct reference regarding the benefits to acknowledging our wrongdoing either to God or to others:

God will be faithful to forgive and cleanse us.	Jeremiah 3:12-13
We will find mercy from God for renouncing our sin.	1 John 1:9
We will find healing from confessing our sin.	Proverbs 28:13
God will turn His anger away from us.	James 5:16

A person who will not confess his or her sin is a foolish person. Pride is at the center of every sin we commit against one another or against God. Pride is what caused Satan to be cast out of heaven as he wanted to be equal with God. We want control. We want to be our own judge of right and wrong and motives. Pride keeps us from our healing because it believes that humbling ourselves and admitting our wrongdoing would give the other person the ability to possibly hurt us or reject our humble behavior. Therefore, we refuse to do what God asks of us because we believe that nothing could be worse than feeling the disdain of another human being.

What does Isaiah 61:3 tell us that God wants our lives to be for Him? Choose one:

A display of His splendor

A picture of grace

A sweet-smelling aroma

List the two requirements of reconciliation we learned from day one and two of this week's homework:

1) ____

2) ____

In order to be truly reconciled to someone where sin has caused a breach in the relationship, we must be secure in God's love. We also have to be willing to restore, or give for the first time, favor and respect for one another which creates the ability to trust where trust has been trampled on or destroyed.

Joseph's brothers had fabricated a message which they sent to Joseph hoping he would continue to show mercy to them after Jacob's death. Their apology was not direct. They shrouded their confession around the guise that Jacob had desired Joseph to continue to treat them well after his death. Their actions caused Joseph to weep.

Have you ever received an apology that rang hollow to you? If yes, share the reason it fell short of feeling like an apology:

A sincere apology will mean different things to different people. I highly recommend the book, *The Five Languages of Apology: How to Experience Healing in all Your Relationships* by Gary Chapman and Jennifer Chapman. Their book explains that we may have received a sincere apology from the person who wronged us, but that our offender did not give an apology in the language/ style we wanted to hear. I have tried to play the role of the sincerity police, a place which is dangerous in encouraging a haughty spirit in me. When we do not hear an apology in the way that speaks to our hearts, but one has still been offered, we must remember the words of Christ and check our own hearts:

So watch yourselves. "If your brother sins, rebuke him, and if he repents, forgive him. If he sins against you seven times in a day, and seven times comes back to you and says, 'I repent,' forgive him." ***Luke 17:3-4***

Nowhere in the above passage does Christ leave room for our judging of the other person's motives or level of sincerity. You and I are commanded to forgive. Period. If our offender has returned to us and has said, "I repent," we are to forgive him or her, even if his or her actions do not seem to be in line with repentance. We must leave the person's motives with God.

What does the apostle Paul urge us to remember in 1 Corinthians 4:5?

It's all going to be shown in the light of God's perfect judgment, my dear friend. We do not have to try to discern the motives of others because our God is doing that with perfect justice. One day, it will all be exposed, including my own impure motives. I need to let mercy triumph over judgment because of that reality!

Let's continue to read Genesis 50:18-21.

What did the brothers tell Joseph they were willing to be to him in verse 18?

I looked up the definition of the word *slave* in the *World English Dictionary*. These are the definitions I found:

1. *a person legally owned by another and having no freedom of action or right to property*
2. *a person who is forced to work for another against his will*
3. *a person under the domination of another person or some habit or influence: a slave to television*
4. *a person who works in harsh conditions for low pay*[3]

Wisdom and patience will serve us far better in the end than being judges of others' character and motives.

Tell me, ladies, in a relationship in which both persons are secure in God's love for them and mutual respect is both given and received, would the words of the brothers in verse 18 be spoken by one friend to another? The brothers' guilty consciences had skewed their view of Joseph's motives behind the kindness he had shown them and had prevented true reconciliation with their brother from happening.

After reading Proverbs 19:11, how does this verse help us to understand Joseph's response to his brothers' fabrication and fear in Genesis 50:21?

Solomon was absolutely right! Wisdom and understanding must be gotten at any cost (see Proverbs 4:7), even when that hard-won wisdom and understanding is achieved in us by wrestling through the misconceptions of others that cause us great pain. Wisdom and patience will serve us far better in the end than being judges of others' character and motives.

Sin must be confronted, however. Let's read Genesis 50:19-20 together:

19 But Joseph said to them, "Don't be afraid. Am I in the place of God? 20 You intended to harm me, but God intended it for good to accomplish what is now being done, the saving of many lives."

Joseph acknowledged his place of power in his brothers' lives in the context of his own position to God. This knowledge will restrain us, dear sister, when we are tempted to continue the viciousness of perpetrating sin against someone who has humbled themselves before us. We are not in the place of God! He has allowed what has happened to us for our good, to prosper us, and to give us a future and a hope (Jeremiah 29:11). Joseph did not dare question God's position of authority even over God's allowance of such deep pain in his life. Are you and I stuck there? Have we refused to let God be sovereign over all that has happened to us, including our most painful moments? How is it working for us to be bitter against Him for the evils that have been perpetrated against us by others? Have we withheld our hearts from Him in some way because we are angry with the One whom Scripture declares to be unsearchable in His judgments and have no counselor His equal (Romans 11:33-34)?

Write out Genesis 50:20 and underline the intentions of the brothers toward Joseph and write them out here:

Now go back and circle how God redeemed the intentions of the brothers and write out how their evil actions were instead used by God:

God, in His unfathomable and infinite mind, knew that the covenant He gave to Abraham to bless all nations through Abraham's descendants would come through the child of promise, Isaac, who was born to Abraham at age one hundred. God knew that the second generation of the covenant would struggle with infertility also and give birth to just two sons. Only one of those sons, Jacob, would receive the covenantal blessing of Abraham, despite his father's plan to give the blessing to his older brother, Esau. God was aware of Jacob's sin of blatant favoritism of Joseph and of the evil his ten older brothers committed against him.

Satan knew that God would be faithful to His promise to Abraham, who would ultimately be the ancestor of the Messiah, Jesus Christ. In each of the four generations of the family of Abraham, he tried his best to destroy the family through whom the Salvation of the world would come. Joseph was not a patriarch as Abraham, Isaac, and Jacob were. Joseph was the preserver of the line of the patriarchs. The fledging family numbered seventy in total, living among a perverse and unholy people in Canaan. Joseph was sent ahead to provide protection from the wicked influences of Canaan, as well as provide sustenance for the family during the world-wide famine.

Satan knew that God would be faithful to His promise to Abraham, who would ultimately be the ancestor of the Messiah, Jesus Christ. In each of the four generations of the family of Abraham, he tried his best to destroy the family through whom the Salvation of the world would come.

Satan was allowed to hurt Joseph in a way that cut him to the very heart. Joseph could have been destroyed by bitterness and hatred toward his brothers. He could have refused to take part in God's plan of redemption and salvation for his family. No human being's limited understanding would fault him if Joseph's decision had been not to cooperate with God. But Joseph, because of his obedience, was able to take part in a plan in which only God could have had the wisdom to be the author. Joseph understood that his pain was for a purpose far bigger than his own life. His obedience through suffering preserved not only those of his generation, but countless others throughout the centuries who would call on the name of Jesus Christ for their salvation.

A contrite and broken heart is one that our God does not despise (Psalm 51:17). A repentant confession maybe the missing piece we need to experience full reconciliation with the one who has hurt us or that we have wounded. I pray with all of my heart that we are willing to make this requirement of reconciliation happen, either as the gracious receiver of the confession or its humble giver.

What, my darling friend, could our forgiveness toward others mean for all eternity? How will future generations be affected that we do not yet know if Jesus does not return in our lifetimes? We must reframe our pain! Even if we never receive a repentant confession from the one who has hurt us so deeply, this is what we must remind ourselves in our struggle to persevere:

Now to him who is able to do immeasurably more than all we ask or imagine, according to his power that is at work within us, to him be glory in the church and in Christ Jesus throughout all generations, for ever and ever! Amen.

– Ephesians 3:20

Joseph understood that his pain was for a purpose far bigger than his own life.

Day 4 – A Heart at Rest

We are almost at the end of our time together in God's Word! I do not work with an outline other than the one in my head, so I learn as I write. It is amazing for me to look back and see how God has led over the past eight weeks of homework. This is my second study and I can tell you that I have prayed over and over again that the Holy Spirit would be our teacher. It is an incredible responsibility to teach God's Word. The enemy has thrown every kind of accusatory dart at me that I am not qualified in the least to do this. I completely agree that I am inadequate, but the One who lives in me is greater than my accuser. I pray that the Holy Spirit would sift these words and bring glory to our only wise God through them.

We are going to cover the last five verses in the book of Genesis today and tomorrow. I have prayed fervently that we would be different women for the time we have spent looking at the life of a family who was used by God in such miraculous ways, despite their glaring dysfunction. I have been honored to have you with me on this journey and would love to hear how God has spoken to you personally through His Word over these eight weeks of study.

Let's read Genesis 20:22-24 for today's reading and answer the following questions:
Where did Joseph and his brothers live after their father died? Circle one:

Canaan Egypt Jerusalem Zion

What are we told about Egyptians regarding how they viewed Joseph's brothers' nationality and occupation according to Genesis 43:32 and Genesis 46:34?

I have prayed fervently that we would be different women for the time we have spent looking at the life of a family who was used by God in such miraculous ways, despite their glaring dysfunction.

In reading through several commentaries, I discovered that the reasons for the cultural prejudices of the Egyptians toward Joseph's family were twofold. First, Egypt had almost been destroyed by the oppressive rule of lawless, wandering marauders called Hycsos, or shepherd-kings. They had been expelled from the land, but only after committing horrible atrocities against the Egyptians. Shepherds were spurned by the Egyptians for another reason: they raised animals for food that the Egyptians worshiped, which was abominable to their religious beliefs.[4]

What does Genesis 38:2 tell us about the nationality of Judah's wife?

What happened to Judah's two older sons who were once married to Tamar according to Genesis 38:7-10?

We are not told specifically why they died, but other passages of the Bible may give us an idea. List the practices the Canaanites were involved in that caused God to destroy them through the Israelites according to Deuteronomy 18:10-12:

Judah and Simeon (see Genesis 46:10) had already intermarried with a people who were wicked in God's sight. We have seen the profound effect parents have on their offspring in this study. All of the practices the Canaanites were involved in had to do with the occult and satanic rituals, the antithesis of anything that was holy or righteous. Left in Canaan, this small family group in number could have adopted and been swallowed up in the culture of Canaan, and leaving the way of their fathers, Abraham, Isaac, and Jacob.

What did God promise Abraham in Genesis 15:5?

God used the Egyptian's disdain for intermingling with the Hebrews as a protection for Jacob's family against the evil influences of the Canaanites. The number that initially arrived in Egypt, grew from a family of seventy members to well over a million people by the time He delivered the descendants of Jacob from Egypt and started them back on the journey to the land he had promised them in Canaan (see Exodus 12:37-38). God's plan works in the midst of human failures. His purposes are firm throughout all generations and are not stopped or thwarted because of evil. The brothers' hatred and jealousy of Joseph did not halt God's plan to take a people for Himself and grow them into a nation that continues to thrive to this day. How much better it is for everyone when all people cooperate who are involved in His amazing plans without damaging one another with sinful choices, of which He is the Redeemer.

How old was Joseph when he died? Underline the correct response:

Sixty-two years Seventy-five years One hundred ten years

One hundred ten years was considered the ideal age to die by the ancient Egyptians![5] Amazing, isn't it, how God is so into the details and bringing Himself glory by being magnificent in front of a people who do not acknowledge Him for themselves.

What does Genesis 50:23 reveal about how many generations Joseph lived to see of his own offspring?

Let's remind ourselves of Joseph's birth order. Leah had four biological sons and then stopped having children for a time. Rachel started a competition with her sister, Leah, when Rachel became a mother through her servant, Bilhah. Leah thought Rachel's plan would work for her as well. The next son born to Leah was through her servant, Zilpah. Bilhah and Zilpah both acted as surrogate mothers for each sister once again as two more sons born to each respectively. And, finally, two more biological sons and a daughter, Dinah, were born to Leah before Rachel delivered Joseph as Jacob's eleventh son.

Whom did Joseph call to him as he was dying according to Genesis 50:24?

Some theologians believe that Joseph was one of the first of his brothers to die, even though he had ten older brothers. Abraham lived to be 175 years old. Isaac was 180 when he died, and Jacob was 147 years old when he breathed his last. Joseph was outlived in years by Jacob by nearly four decades. Scripture does not tell us why Joseph's life was significantly shorter than the three generations of men in his family that lived before him.

Charles Haddon Spurgeon is one of my favorite theologians. I have several volumes of his sermons along with a set of his commentaries on the Psalms. He was born in England in 1834 and died in 1892 at the age of fifty-seven years. When my heart is broken, I often go to his writings to see how the Lord spoke through him. I have yet to walk away without feeling encouraged and uplifted by the obvious anointing the Holy Spirit had on Spurgeon's thoughts and sermons.

I have often thought of how young Spurgeon was when he died. I sometimes wonder why God takes godly men and women home to be with Him long before their biological age would pronounce them to be old. I do believe that there are some men and women of God of whom "this world is not worthy" (see Hebrews 11:38).

I do believe that there are some men and women of God of whom "this world is not worthy"

What does Isaiah 57:1-2 tell us?

Do you know anyone personally who believed in Christ for salvation and died young? How do the above verses give insight as to possibly why that person was taken home to be with Jesus?

My grandfather, Dr. Laban Smith, found Christ when he was in his late thirties. He was a very successful oral surgeon who had everything one could want in the way of worldly success. He did not consider matters of eternity until his first wife, Ruby, died of a brain tumor. Desperate to find answers to his deepest questions, he attended a small chapel service where the good news of Jesus Christ was explained to him and knew immediately that he needed a Savior. He married my grandmother, Marcella, a few years later and, five years into their marriage, he decided to sell his dental practices and board a ship called the *Jean Jadot* for a new life as a missionary with my grandmother in the Belgian Congo. Fifteen years later, at the height of their ministry among former cannibals, he fell and broke his neck and died, leaving my grandmother a widow with two young boys to raise alone. My grandfather was fifty-five years old.

I believe that Charles Spurgeon, my grandfather, and Joseph all shared a similar experience. Each one of them experienced suffering at different points in their lives, but there was something that each of them possessed at the end of their lives which eludes many people, even those who profess Christ as Savior. They each had a heart that was at rest. Peace is something that cannot be bought. We can strive continually and never find the one thing we truly desire that will bring us the most joy – peace that comes from knowing where our security lies. At the end of his life, Joseph was not burdened by chains of bitterness caused by withholding forgiveness from those who had hurt him the most.

Reconciliation comes when both parties can trust God to maintain our lot for us.

What truth in Psalm 16:5 had Joseph learned through his wrestling with God over what had happened to him?

I love how the Amplified Bible translate the last part of Psalm 16:5: *You hold and maintain my lot.*

Reconciliation comes when both parties can trust God to maintain our lot for us. He has assigned our portion and our cup. Psalm 16 is a Messianic psalm. That cup that is referred to was the same cup of suffering that the Father chose for his beloved Son, Jesus Christ, to drink. That cup that Jesus asked to be allowed to pass without Him drinking it contained the most bitter pain and anguish any human being has ever suffered, but Jesus knew that God the Father could be trusted to raise Him from the dead once again.

Two people who have wounded each other badly will find the healing of reconciliation when both can be at rest. Suspicion no longer raises its ugly head at every turn. We no longer assume that the other meant us harm. It can happen, my dear friend! My life is a walking, breathing testimony to the fact that Jesus can take a family relationship once marred by jealousy and hurt and reconcile two hearts by His miraculous grace.

[4] Love is patient, love is kind. It does not envy, it does not boast, it is not proud. [5] It is not rude, it is not self-seeking, it is not easily angered, it keeps no record of wrongs. [6] Love does not delight in evil but rejoices with the truth. [7] It always protects, always trusts, always hopes, always perseveres.
– 1 Corinthians 13:4-7

List reconciliation's requirements from days 1-4 here:

After reading these verses on the definition of love, ask the Holy Spirit to help you discern what He might be asking you to do to become a person whose heart is at rest and share your thoughts below.

I am so proud of your perseverance!

Day 5 – A View of the Eternal

I cannot tell you how thrilled I am over the persistant and difficult work you have done in the last eight weeks of this study. I do not think that any week has been particularly lighthearted or could be characterized as fun. This has been the first in-depth study for some of you. I wish you could see the joy in my face as I have started to type this last lesson of study on the life of Joseph and his family. Goodbyes are never easy for me. I have always been a lover of great stories. I have been known to read the same book or watch the same movie over and over again. I pray that you will read Genesis 12-50 with a new feeling of familiarity the next time you open this portion of Scripture. Of one thing I am certain – we will never exhaust the lessons that are contained in these chapters even if we read the verses written there every day for the rest of our lives.

What do the following Scriptures tell us about the Word of God?

Psalm 19:9, 11:

Psalm 119:89:

Luke 21:33:

John 17:17:

My dear sisters, how many people in this world would love to be involved in something that is eternal?

My dear sisters, how many people in this world would love to be involved in something that is eternal? We read stories everyday about the foolishness of some who have compromised the sacred for fifteen minutes of fame. When we make time to study the Word of God, we invest in what is eternal. God's Word will never pass away. May we love His Word more than anything else we possess. The Holy Spirit will help us remember what we have been taught by Scripture. I am amazed at how He will bring back to my memory a verse that had been buried in my mind for months or even years at just the right moment to convict, protect, comfort, or strengthen me. His Word will never return void, but will accomplish what He sent it for, perhaps long after this study is over (Isaiah 55:10-11).

What did Solomon say in Ecclesiastes 7:8? Share what you think this means:

There is nothing to signal an ending quite like a funeral. You and I are going to be attending a funeral today in the last two verses of the last chapter we will study in the book of Genesis. I have attended a few funerals in my lifetime, most of them were for friends and family that have put their trust in Jesus Christ. Amidst the intense sorrow, there has been a glimmer of hope that has permeated the somberness of the moment as the last earthly goodbye is said.

We have been talking about reconciliation's requirements throughout this week of study. It is my prayer that this final lesson will prove Solomon's words to be true in a way that will give us hope as we persevere and continue to forgive, even if the fulfillment of reconciliation's requirements seems impossible to us at this moment.

Let's remind ourselves of what those requirements are from days one through four of this week's homework. Fill in the following blanks:

1) Belief in a love that surpasses ____________________________.
2) A mutual _____________________.
3) A ____________________________ confession.
4) A heart at ___________________.

What do we do if reconciliation seems impossible in this lifetime? What if we, like Joseph, have forgiven, but the other party will not take us up on the forgiveness we offer? What if suspicion and a presumption of harm continue to make life difficult to be in a relationship with someone?

After reading Hebrews 11:13-16, let's answer the following questions:

We must have an eternal perspective.

What was the dilemma of the persons written about in verse 13?

What were they looking for in verse 14?

What was the reward by God of their tenacious faith in verse 16?

It makes me want to weep and renew my commitment once again to doing the hard and painful process of forgiving, even when reconciliation seems out of reach. Let's read Genesis 50:24-25.

Whom did Joseph tell his brothers would rescue them and help them in verse 24?

The brothers had been terrified after their father's death that Joseph was going to hold a grudge against them and seek revenge for the evil they had done against them. Even on his deathbed, Joseph clung to the promise that we all must believe by faith, my dear sister, if we are going to not just survive this life, but thrive in the abundant life that Jesus has promised is yours and mine: We must have an eternal perspective.

Proverbs 3:32 tells us that, *"the Lord hates a perverse man, but takes the upright into His confidence."* This is the only explanation I have for these words of prophecy that Joseph spoke in Genesis 50:24. Joseph had no Bible, ladies! Moses would not write the first five books of the Old Testament for more than four hundred years!

What further instructions did Joseph give his brothers in Genesis 50:25?

The promise of God Himself aiding the family that would be left on earth was repeated by Joseph again in verse 25. With the eyes of faith, Joseph understood what his brothers never did! His pain had profound purpose for bringing about the plans of God that stood firm eternally, despite Satan's greatest attempt to destroy those plans. Joseph's choice to be obedient would ultimately lead to the birth of God's one and only perfect Son, Jesus Christ, the Savior of the world.

What further insight does Hebrews 11:22 give us about Joseph's knowledge?

Wait and hope for and expect the Lord; be brave and of good courage and let your heart be stout and enduring. Yes, wait for and hope for and expect the Lord.
– Psalm 27:14 (AMP)

Joseph knew that horrible suffering was going to happen to his family in Egypt because God had taken him into His confidence. There was no more powerful a testament to the faithfulness of God than Joseph's life to remind future generations that God would not be thwarted in His promise to bring them back to Canaan, despite the bondage they would one day face.

Can you and I believe our Jesus could do something so magnificent with our pain? Could we dare to ask for eyes of faith to believe Him for the opportunity to be involved in His plan for us that would supersede anything we could ask or imagine? Could we praise Him for the perseverance He promises us that He is using to make us mature and complete, not lacking anything (James 1:2-4)?

[What, what would have become of me] had I not believed I would see the goodness of the Lord in the land of the living! Wait and hope for and expect the Lord; be brave and of good courage and let your heart be stout and enduring. Yes, wait for and hope for and expect the Lord.
– Psalm 27:13-14 (Amplified Bible)

How, my precious friend, is Jesus speaking to you through the verses above in your struggle to live out forgiveness?

What does Genesis 50:26 tell us about Joseph's remains?

These are the words of Matthew Henry regarding this final verse in Genesis:

[Joseph] was put in a coffin in Egypt, but not buried till his children had received their inheritance in Canaan.[6]

For four hundred thirty years, Joseph's coffin was a reminder to the children of Israel that they could wait in expectation for God to come to their aid and return them back to the promised land of Canaan God swore on oath to Abraham. Did you ever realize that the day the Israelites set out from their bondage in Egypt that Joseph's bones went with them? When the Israelites saw the mighty waves of the Red Sea held back by Jehovah's power, Joseph's bones crossed over with them on dry land. Throughout the intense heat of forty years of wandering through the desert with Moses because of the older generation's unbelief and grumbling against Jehovah, Joseph's bones reminded that generation's children that God would do what He said He would do.

As the mighty walls of Jericho fell under Joshua's command, Joseph's coffin continued to remind the Israelites of the man who had conquered his desire for revenge and had left his pain with the Redeemer. Almost five hundred years after Joseph prophesied what God had revealed to him, his bones were laid to rest in the land promised to Abraham, Isaac, and Jacob.

Listen to what Charles Spurgeon says about Joseph's reward in Canaan:

And, to finish, God gave Joseph and his family a double portion in Israel, which never happened to any other of the 12 sons of Jacob. Jacob said, "And now your two sons, Ephraim and Manasseh, which were born unto you in the land of Egypt before I came unto you into Egypt are mine; as Reuben and Simeon they shall be mine," thus making each of them into a tribe. Ephraim and Manasseh each stood at the head of a tribe as if they had been actually sons of Jacob! Levi is taken out of the 12 and provision is made for the Levites as servants of God. And then Ephraim and Manasseh are put in, so that Joseph's house figures twice among the twelve! There are two Josephs in Israel but only one Judah! Joseph has a double portion of the kingdom![7]

After reading Joshua 24:32, what details about Joseph's final earthly resting place stand out to you and why?

Shechem was the place of shame and grief and utter brutality for the family caused by Dinah's rape and her brothers' fury. What does Job 11:15-16 tell us?

Sometimes, reconciliation is not possible in this lifetime because only one person wants to do the difficult work it requires, my dear sister. Forgiveness, however, is always possible because forgiveness can be accomplished by one person – you. For those of us who are continuing to live with unresolved issues of reconciliation, we must persevere in prayer that our almighty God would do a work in the hearts of all who may be involved so that He can bring glory to Himself. Our job is to trust and obey in the wait and live in such a way that we bring honor to the One who took our shame upon Himself on a cross He did not deserve.

As we end our time together, I wanted us to remind ourselves of what is ahead for those who have made Jesus our Savior. We have spent the majority of our study in the first book of our Bibles. We are going to end our time in the magnificent Word of God by discovering the reward we will be given if we continue to keep an eternal view during the difficulties we encounter in our relationships here on earth.

I stayed away from the book of Revelation because I felt so inadequate to understand the prophecies contained in its chapters. I still have many questions, but the chapter that you and I are going to look at is full of profound hope. I pray that the Lord would deeply encourage us as we read this passage.

Forgiveness, however, is always possible because forgiveness can be accomplished by one person – you.

We are going to end by reading portions of Revelation 21. Please read verses 1-5 and record how the Holy Spirit is speaking to you in this passage:

After reading verses 9-14, whose names are written on the gates mentioned in verse 12?

My dear sisters, the brothers who perhaps never saw reconciliation on earth will stand together for all eternity because their names are engraved on the gates of the Holy City of the New Jerusalem. Why is this so? We have to read on in verses 22-27.

What does Revelation 21: 27 specifically say?

The ministry of reconciliation will take place, my dear friend, either here on earth or in heaven for those who have trusted Christ as Savior. No longer will we do anything impure, shameful, or deceitful to one another. There will be no more suspicion, no desire for revenge, and no misunderstanding ever again for the glory of God will be our one and only desire. We will worship Him in perfect unity and truth. What a glorious day awaits us!

As we close the last day of study, I pray with all my heart that you and I would continue to obey our Jesus and forgive others as He has commanded us. What does 1 John 3:2 promise us we will one day be? Circle one:

Clean before our God

We will be like Him

Perfect in our thoughts

I can hardly wrap my mind around that magnificent truth! I can think of no better way than to end this study than with the words of the apostle Peter:

In this you greatly rejoice, though now for a little while you may have had to suffer grief in all kinds of trials. These have come so that your faith – of greater worth than gold, which perishes even though refined by fire – may be proved genuine and may result in praise, glory and honor when Jesus Christ is revealed. Though you have not seen him, you love him; and even though you do not see him now, you believe in him and are filled with an inexpressible and glorious joy, for you are receiving the goal of your faith, the salvation of your souls. ***– 1 Peter 1:6-9***

My love and my prayers for you, my dear friend, as God helps us to see this harvest in our lives!

My darling friend,

Before you were born, your Creator planned out a life for you that would ultimately lead you to Jesus Christ. You may have been raised in church and have tried to live a good life. You also may be exhausted and disillusioned with having to try to be good enough to be worthy of love. Until you have settled the most important question you will ever wrestle with, your heart will continue to search for something or someone in this world that can never fill the void you know is there.

I want to share with you the best news you will ever hear. You are deeply loved by a God whose love for you is unfailing and unconditional. You do not have to do anything to make yourself worthy of this love. You only need to accept the gift of salvation he offers to you through His Son, Jesus Christ.

The apostle Paul was inspired by the Holy Spirit to write the following truth:

"That if you confess with your mouth, "Jesus is Lord," and believe in your heart that God raised him from the dead, you will be saved. For it is with your heart that you believe and are justified, and it is with your mouth that you confess and are saved. As the Scripture says, "Anyone who trusts in him will never be put to shame."
Romans 10:9-11

Do you want the abundant life that Jesus Christ offers in John 10:10 to all who believe on Him for salvation? The first step toward that life is in asking Jesus Christ to become your Savior. He doesn't want a perfect life to be surrendered to Him. He will accept you as you are. If you are ready to have Jesus be the Lord of your life, please pray this simple prayer:

God,

I know that I am a sinner. I believe that Jesus Christ died on the cross for my sins and that you have raised Him from the dead. I want to surrender my life to the Lordship of Jesus Christ from this point on. Thank you for saving me and for loving me with a love that will never fail me. Give me a desire for You and Your will that surpasses any other desire I have in my life.

In Jesus' Name,

Amen

May I have the privilege of welcoming you as my sister in Christ? Please tell a fellow Christian what you have done and get involved in a Bible-believing church. I cannot tell you how thrilled I am over your decision. I would love to hear about how the Lord brought you to Himself at esengoministries@aol.com. God bless you!

End Notes

Week One: Uncovering the Poison

1 Santayana, George. *The Life of Reason, Volume 1.* New York: Prometheus Books, 1998.

2 Pink, Arthur. *Gleanings in Genesis.* Stilwell: Digireads.com Publishing, 2005.

3 Epp, Theodore. *The God of Jacob.* Lincoln: The Good News Broadcasting Association, 1983.

Week Two: A House Divided

1 "A House Divided." Abraham Lincoln Online: Speeches and Writings. 2011. 1 August 2011. <http://showcase.netins.net/web/creative/lincoln/speeches/house.htm>.

2 Pink, Arthur. *Gleanings in Genesis.* Stilwell: Digireads.com Publishing, 2005.

3 Epp, Theodore. *The God of Jacob.* Lincoln: The Good News Broadcasting Association, 1983.

Week Three: A Hard Journey Home

1 "deceit." Merriam-Webster Online Dictionary. 2011. Merriam-Webster Online. 3 February 2011<http://www.merriam-webster.com/dictionary/deceit>.

2 Henry, Matthew. "Commentary on Genesis 30". *Matthew Henry Complete Commentary on the Whole Bible.* 15 February 2011. http://www.biblestudytools.com/commentaries/matthew-henry-complete/genesis/30.html?p=4

3 "vow." Merriam-Wester Online Dictionary. 2011. Merriam-Webster Online. 15 February 2011<http://www.merriam-webster.com/dictionary/vow>.

4 Henry, Matthew. "Commentary on Genesis 35". *Matthew Henry Complete Commentary on the Whole Bible.* 15 February 2011. http://www.biblestudytools.com/commentaries/matthew-henry-complete/genesis/35.html

5 "Allon Bakuth." *Strong's Exhaustive Concordance: New American Standard Bible.* Updated ed. La Habra: Lockman Foundation, 1995. Bible Study Tools Online. Web. 20 February 2011.

6 Tindley, Charles. "Nothing Between." Timeless Truths Free Online Library. 5 March 2011.<http://library.timelesstruths.org/music/Nothing_Between/>

Week Four: Trail of Tears

1 Schmutzer, Andrew. "Genesis - Vol. 2: Joseph's Departure and Judah's Sin." Moody Bible Institute, Chicago. 2009. Lecture.

2 "The Wisdom of God." *Living on the Edge With Chip Ingram.* Moody Radio. WFCM, Murfreesboro. 4 April 2011.

3 Schmutzer, Andrew. "Genesis - Vol. 2: Joseph's Three Jobs." Moody Bible Institute, Chicago. 2009. Lecture.

Week Five: Dark Night of the Soul

1 Youngblood, Ronald, et. al., *Nelson's New Illustrated Bible Dictionary.* (Nashville: Thomas Nelson Publishers, 1995),134.

2 Spurgeon, Charles. "Psalm 105:19: Trial By the Word." Metropolitan Tabernacle Sermons. 7 March 2011. www. spurgeon.org/sermons/1277.htm

3 Ibid, 1277. www. spurgeon.org/sermons/1277.htm.

Week Six: High Places

1 Youngblood, Ronald, et. al., *Nelson's New Illustrated Bible Dictionary.* (Nashville: Thomas Nelson Publishers, 1995), 896.

2 Schmutzer, Dr. Andrew. "Genesis - Vol. 2: Joseph's Brothers Arrive." Moody Bible Institute, Chicago. 2009. Lecture.

3 Schmutzer, Dr. Andrew. "Genesis - Vol. 2: Joseph Tests His Brothers." Moody Bible Institute, Chicago. 2009. Lecture.

Week Seven: The Plan of Glory

1 "C.S. Lewis Quotes." Goodreads.com. 2008. 5 April 2011. <http://www.goodreads.com/quotes/show/3058>.

2 "Matthew 7:6." Christnotes.org. 2011. 5 April 2011. <http://www.christnotes.org/commentary.php?com=wes&b=40&c=7.>

3 Schmutzer, Dr. Andrew. "Genesis - Vol. 2: Joseph Reveals His Identity." Moody Bible Institute, Chicago. 2009. Lecture.

4 Schmutzer, Dr. Andrew. "Genesis - Vol. 2: Israel's Exodus to Egypt." Moody Bible Institute, Chicago. 2009. Lecture.

Week Eight: Reconciliation's Requirements

1 "Reconciliation." *Strong's Exhaustive Concordance: New American Standard Bible.* Updated ed. La Habra: Lockman Foundation, 1995. Bible Study Tools Online. Web. 3 August 2011.

2 Schmutzer, Dr. Andrew. "Genesis - Vol. 2: Israel's Exodus to Egypt." Moody Bible Institute, Chicago. 2009. Lecture.

3 "slave." *World English Dictionary.* 2011. World English Dictionary Online. 5 August 2011. <http://dictionary.reference.com/browse/slave>.

4 "Genesis 43:32." *Adam Clarke's Commentary on the Bible.* 1831. Biblios.com. Web. 8 August 2011. <http://clarke.biblecommenter.com/genesis/43.htm>.

5 Bruce, F.F., *New International Bible Commentary.* (Grand Rapids: Zondervan Publishing House, 1979), 147.

6 Henry, Matthew. "Commentary on Genesis 50". *Matthew Henry Complete Commentary on the Whole Bible.* 8 August 2011. <http://www.biblestudytools.com/commentaries/matthew-henry-complete/genesis/50.html?p=4>.

7 Spurgeon, Charles. "A Miniature Portrait of Joseph." Metropolitan Tabernacle Sermons. 9 August 2011. <http://www.spurgeongems.org/vols25-27/chs1610.pdf>.

NOTES